sugar

sugar

SIMPLE SWEETS AND DECADENT DESSERTS

ANNA OLSON

whitecap

Edited by Alison Maclean
Proofread by Marial Shea
Design by Roberta Batchelor
Photography by Christopher Freeland
Food styling by Claire Stubbs

Whitecap Books and the author would like to thank Caban and
The Cook's Place in Toronto for supplying the following props for photography:
Caban:
   Blueberry Buckle: side plate, dinner plate
   Butterscotch Bars with Chai Coffee: glass mug, plate
   Chocolate Chip Cookies: napkin
   Cashew Cookie Platter: platter
   Raspberry Cardamom Cobbler: cappuccino cup, saucer
   Rhubarb Cream Tart: side plates
   Pineapple Carrot Mini Cakes: square plate, fork, napkin
The Cook's Place:
   Petits Fours: rectangular platter
   Coffee and Doughnuts: square platter
All other props are privately owned.

Printed and bound in Canada

NATIONAL LIBRARY OF CANADA CATALOGUING IN PUBLICATION

Olson, Anna, 1968-
   Sugar: simple sweets and decadent desserts/Anna Olson.

   Includes index.
   ISBN 1-55285-509-0

   1. Desserts. I. Title.
TX773.O46 2004   641.8'6   C2004-900370-4

The publisher acknowledges the financial support of the Government of Canada through the Book Publishing Industry Development Program for our publishing activities.

Acknowledgements

✧ ✧ ✧ I would like to thank my husband, Michael, for his constant love and encouragement, and for teaching me to laugh heartily at my mistakes. And loving thanks to my stepdaughter Mika, for keeping all of us young in spirit.

I would like to thank my parents for their loving support and patience in listening to all my wacky ideas.

A special posthumous wish of gratitude has to be given to Julia Hajzak (Grandma) and Mary Adamjak (Nan), who were my role models for baking with love, patience and a smile. They are always in my thoughts when I am in the kitchen.

Also deserving of thanks is Alison Maclean. I wish I could have an editor for all my daily tasks — life would be far simpler (and grammatically correct).

Any many, many thanks go to all the staff of Sugar including Heather Ryall, Holly Gillanders, Claudia Bianchi, Patti Heatherington, Lucie Gilchrist and most especially Tanya Linton. They are an inspiring group of women and I have had such a memorable time working and laughing with them. Sugar babes rule!

Introduction

◇ ◇ ◇ It's astounding how much we love desserts and sugar — so much so that we use sugar's descriptors to endear others; I call my husband "sweetie" and "honey" regularly, and in return I am "cookie" (even "cookie-face," I dare confess). We "sugar" our language when trying to be gentle or tender as opposed to "peppering" our phrases with expletives. Sweets of any variety seem to wake up quite emotive responses, even carnal at times (you know what they say about chocolate and vanilla)! My passion for desserts reaches beyond mere indulgence — I love making them.

My grandmother, Julia Hajzak, was my first inspiration for cooking and baking. She took great pride in the meals she cooked for us and spent minimal time at the kitchen table enjoying the food because she would be up by the stove refilling platters and bowls and checking that we were all sated. Christmastime was always exciting; I would help with the Christmas cookies and also learn a lot about our Slovak culinary heritage (the polar opposite of the currently popular low-carbohydrate diets). As Grandma's memory began to fade, we were still always able to talk recipes, and the sparkle would return to her eye as she could recall with clarity cooking and baking with her own mother. Of course these recipes were never in cups and ounces, just "add enough flour until it feels right" and "bake it until it's done." It is these recipes that have become the blueprint for my culinary personality. I share her joy for baking, which translates to a joy in sharing with others.

That is what is so fantastic about baking and desserts — the joy of sharing. When we decide to bake something as simple as a batch of chocolate chip cookies, or as ornate as a Bavarian Torte, we do it not just for our own satisfaction, but because we want to share with others (all right, there is the rare occasion when I feel like eating the whole batch of cookie dough myself!). Never will we find a dessert recipe that states "**serves** 1." For me, success is when I watch my family or guests take that first bite, pause for a split second, then hum and smile at the same time.

I find a secondary satisfaction in baking, and that is in the technical mastery. Probably one of the more scientific arms of the culinary body, baking has a text of tools and rules that are not meant to intimidate — quite the opposite in fact. These general rules in baking are intended to lead us to success. I found in my education that after I learned how to bake and came to understand how sugar behaves when heated, and what eggs do, and how glutens in flour work, and so on, that my savoury cooking improved tremendously. I also became a little more creative, letting my baking and pastry skills spill into my other cooking, creating things like Saffron Custards, Horseradish Mousse and Cheddar Shortbread.

My step into the culinary world was a gradual one. Although I grew up with culinary inspiration, it was too inherent for me to see plainly as a career choice. I went to university to study political science, all the while enjoying cooking (and at that time, budgeting), but still without a fixed career plan. After school, I fell into a banking position at a small investment firm in Toronto, and while the other employees would spend their lunch hours perusing annual reports and analyzing indices, I was at the St. Lawrence farmers' market perusing the stalls for whatever was freshest or newest to me. I would have friends over whenever I could, to cook for them. Not always successful, I remember the first Thanksgiving dinner I prepared for my family. I made a spectacular-looking pumpkin pie that proved to be unintentionally sugar-free! I tried pouring maple syrup over it to try to repair the damage, but a good laugh and an extra glass of wine was all that was needed to resolve the situation.

It was not long after the pumpkin pie debacle that I came to my senses and decided to follow a path into cooking professionally. After a particularly rough day at work, I found myself up at 2 a.m. making banana muffins, not to actually eat them, but for the relaxing act of making them. I had my epiphany at that moment and realized that I should cook for a living. I left the world of finance and traveled through the United States for a few months before landing in Vail, Colorado to study culinary arts at Johnson and Wales University.

I gained some experience working in the States, including stints in Fredericksberg, Texas and New Orleans. About ready for a change, I returned to Toronto to visit my parents. They had heard of a marvelous new winery restaurant, On the Twenty, in the Niagara region and suggested we dine there. I was hooked. The use of local and seasonal ingredients prepared honestly and enticingly did just that — entice me to work there. I made the move to Niagara seamlessly in 1995, and have been happily married to my own Prince Charming, Michael, since 1999.

Over the years of working, entertaining and traveling, I have built a substantial repertoire of recipes that feature classic preparations and creative new methods, using fresh, seasonal ingredients wherever possible. I co-wrote the *Inn on the Twenty Cookbook* with Michael, and became comfortable teaching cooking classes and demonstrations, sharing what I know. The next step in sharing my recipes was a grand one — the big world of television.

To be invited to share my personal recipes as host of *sugar*, on Food Network Canada, has been exceptionally gratifying. To me, the greatest compliment is when I hear that someone has not only watched the program, but has made my desserts with success.

As does the television program *sugar*, this cookbook has a distinct personality. Instead of chapters laid out as "cakes," "tarts," "cookies" and so on, I have presented the recipes as you see them on the program. One key ingredient is presented, first in an easy-to-prepare recipe that most likely can be made with ingredients you already have in your pantry. This is great when you need a dessert or sweet in a hurry, or when you feel like spending more time eating it than making it. The second dessert of this key ingredient may be a little more elaborate, but that doesn't mean it is difficult to achieve. These are the showpieces — the desserts to pull out of the fridge or oven to sounds of "ooh" and "aahhh" as you bring them to the table. Many of these desserts can be prepared in advance, and are perfect for entertaining. In addition to the simple recipe, I include a trick or two, the "switch up," to either transform the main recipe effortlessly into another dessert or to dress it up into something you'd be proud to serve to guests.

Along the way, I am going to hold your hand, so to speak. In addition to the concise recipes, I provide many tips and tricks to help guarantee your success. On top of building an impressive dessert, I want you to impress yourself!

These recipes truly do express my culinary personality. I use some classic techniques and flavours, but I also use seasons and senses as inspiration. Using fresh fruit in season is always recommended, and if there's nothing in season, well, there's always chocolate! I also like to build desserts and dessert plates with consideration for the balance of colour, taste and texture.

Please use my recipes as building blocks. I often provide options for substitutions within a recipe, and please take liberties in experimenting in your own kitchen. I choose to bake with unsalted butter, and throughout the body of the book I'll explain why, but it is just that — my choice. If you prefer baking with margarine or shortening, please feel free to continue. Do keep in mind, though, that the proportions of ingredients should remain the same to ensure success.

At the end of the day, what counts is that you enjoy the result of your baking, and also the process of making your dessert. Remember that the sense of accomplishment and the pleasure in baking is calorie-free!

baking basics

INGREDIENTS | TOOLS | TECHNIQUES

Ingredients

BAKING POWDER: Baking powder works as a leavening agent and is activated in two steps. Its combination with liquid initiates the release of carbon dioxide, followed by a second release when heated. Baking powder also has a built-in acidic component to activate, so added acidity is not required, unlike with baking soda. Store well-sealed in a dry place and replace every 6 to 8 months.

BAKING SODA: To work as a leavening agent, baking soda requires an acidic ingredient to activate it, such as vinegar, lemon juice, yoghurt, sour cream or even molasses. Once in contact with this acid, it starts releasing carbon dioxide immediately, so don't dawdle in getting that cake to the oven! Baking soda is also a great tool to remove food burnt onto pots — simply add a tablespoon of baking soda to the scorched pot and cover with water. Simmer for about 15 minutes and stir to pull off the burnt pieces.

Store baking soda well-sealed and in a dry place, but replace often (every 2 months). Fortunately, baking soda is probably one of the cheapest ingredients available!

BROWN SUGAR: There are basically two types of brown sugar — light (or golden) and dark. Light brown sugar has less molasses in it and hence a milder flavour while dark brown sugar has a deeper colour and taste and is also a little heavier. I specify in all my recipes which to use, but no matter which type is called for, the technique for measuring brown sugar remains constant. Be certain to pack the brown sugar into your measuring cup for the most accurate results.

Store your brown sugar in an airtight container with a piece of bread to keep it moist (change the bread every month or so). If your brown sugar does dry out there are two ways to fix it. The quick-fix is simply to microwave your measured amount for about 15 seconds on high while the other trick is to add an apple slice to your sugar canister — in a day your brown sugar will be back to normal (just be sure to replace that apple slice with a piece of bread afterwards).

BUTTER: Without exception I use only unsalted butter in my baking, and I often get asked, "Why?" Unsalted butter gives me, the baker, control over the recipe. Some recipes require a touch of salt and some require quite a bit, but if I am using unsalted butter then I control how much salt is being added to the dish. I find that the salt content of butter varies from brand to brand, and I also find that unsalted butter has a sweeter, fresher taste that translates beautifully into the final baked product.

When I call for chilled or cold butter in a recipe, I mean that it should come directly from the fridge. Cold butter worked into a pastry dough helps produce a tender, even flaky result. If you ever feel during a pastry-making process that your butter is warming, just toss it in the freezer for a few minutes and then resume working with it. Remember that using an electric appliance adds friction and therefore heat to your dough, so sometimes working by hand can be better.

When I call for room-temperature butter, it should be exactly that, 68–72°F (18–21°C). Now, of course I never have the forethought to pull my butter out hours ahead for my baking, so I find it easiest to cut the butter into pieces and soften it in the microwave for 10–20 seconds on medium.

When a recipe calls for melted butter, I measure it first then melt it. It is also important to let the melted butter cool slightly before working it into the recipe.

Store your butter well-wrapped in the refrigerator — those butter-keepers on the fridge door do work well. Dairy products absorb odours quickly, so the butter-keeper keeps unwanted fragrances out!

CHOCOLATE: Your chocolate desserts will only be as good as the chocolate you use. Without naming brands, price generally guides you as to quality and Belgian chocolate has the best reputation. Do not use chocolate chips in place of baking chocolate (otherwise known as couverture) — they will not melt smoothly into desserts.

There are three types of chocolate — dark, milk and white. Dark is divided into two categories — the more common semisweet chocolate and the darker bittersweet chocolate that earns its name as it is less sweet and a little sharper than semisweet. I opt for bittersweet in my recipes, but all will work just fine if you use semisweet. Milk chocolate has less chocolate liqueur (the strong, bitter edge in chocolate) than dark, and has the addition of milk and vanilla. It is now easier to find baking milk chocolate, and if it's not available in your grocery or specialty foods store, try asking your local confectionery if they will sell you some. White chocolate is actually a bit of a misnomer, as there is no chocolate liqueur, but only cocoa butter, milk and vanilla (no wonder it melts on the tip of our tongues!).

Store chocolate well-wrapped in a cool, dark place (but never in the fridge) for up to a year. Sometimes, with temperature fluctuations, chocolate develops a "bloom" on it and turns white on the outside. This does not indicate the chocolate has spoiled — use it as usual.

CITRUS: Lemons, limes and oranges are such a gift in the world of desserts because they offer two flavour-builders — the zest and the juice. Zest is perfect when you want the fragrance and taste of citrus in your desserts without the acidity, and heat draws out the citrus flavour even more. When zesting your fruits, be sure to only remove the coloured part of the fruit — the white pith has a bitter edge.

Citrus juice is great to create a flavour of its own, but also to enhance other flavours. I find that if I have purchased other fruit that may not be at its peak the addition of a little lemon juice with a touch of sugar brings out the taste of that fruit more (strawberries are a perfect example).

Make sure you store your citrus fruits in a separate crisper drawer from your green vegetables. Citrus fruits emit ethylene gases that can brown and wilt green vegetables. Mind you, if you need to ripen an avocado, pear or banana faster, just place them in the same bowl as your citrus fruits.

CREAM: Ah, the goodness of cream! I'd be lost as a pastry chef without it.

The most important rule to remember when making a recipe that calls for whipping cream is only whipping cream will do — no substitutions. Whipping cream has a fat content of 35%, anything below 30% will not whip up to hold air and anything lower in fat will split and curdle if an acid is combined with it.

Have you ever puzzled over how much cream to whip for a dollop on your desserts? Whipped cream has twice the volume of the liquid you start with, so a 2 Tbsp (25 mL) dollop of whipped cream requires 1 Tbsp (15 ml) of liquid cream.

Whipped cream whips best when you start with cold cream and a cold metal or glass bowl (I put it in the freezer for 10 minutes). When a recipe calls for anything less than 1 cup (250 mL), I always do it by hand — it saves pulling out the mixer and I get a little workout at the same time!

EGGS: In all my recipes, when I call for eggs, I am referring to large Grade "A" white eggs. I find that large brown eggs have smaller yolks than the white, so I use those just for breakfast!

A general rule in baking is that the egg in your recipe should be the same temperature as the butter. If you are making pastry dough that calls for cold butter, then use cold eggs. If the butter (or milk, etc.) is at room temperature, then use room-temperature eggs.

Store eggs in their cartons (they are designed for airflow to keep eggs fresh) in the refrigerator until ready to use. To bring them up to room temperature rapidly, immerse them, in their shells, in hot tap water for 3 to 4 minutes.

FLOUR: There are three general types of flour: bread, pastry and all purpose. Bread flour is milled from hearty winter wheat and has a high protein, or gluten, content to give it strength to hold in carbon dioxide that yeast produces as bread rises and bakes. Pastry flour is milled from summer wheat and has a far lower protein content and is milled finer, for more tender cakes and pastries. All purpose flour is quite simply a blend of the two. I tend to use unbleached flours for more predictable results, but I leave that choice up to you.

Store all flours well sealed in a dry place up to a year. Pastry flour is a little more susceptible to moisture than bread or all purpose flour, so if you don't use it often, store it in the freezer.

MILK: As a pastry chef's apprentice, I learned that only whole milk can be used in baked goods. While I still practice this whenever I can, the practical truth is that I always have 2% milk in my fridge, not whole milk. All of my recipes that call for milk work equally well with whole or 2% milk. I do not recommend 1% or skim — there's not enough fat to add body and taste to the recipes. Is 1% what you drink, but you use half-and-half for your coffee? Replace 2 Tbsp (25 mL) of a 1 cup (250 mL) measure of milk with half-and-half cream to create an appropriate whole milk substitute.

MOLASSES: Two types of molasses are used in baking. Fancy molasses is a milder, lighter-coloured style that is perfect in desserts such as gingerbread. Blackstrap molasses is darker and has a bitter edge to it, and is used primarily in bread-baking. I specify fancy molasses in all my recipes. For easier measuring and pouring while baking, lightly oil your liquid measuring cup before adding the molasses — it'll slide right out without messy scraping.

SALT: Salt is such an important part of baking and desserts, even in the sometimes minute amounts you see specified in recipes. Salt balances and tempers flavours; it brings out the depth of chocolate, it cuts the sweetness of sugar and enhances the richness in pastry, and also tempers the leavening power of yeast. I always use finely ground salt, either table or sea salt, in desserts. Kosher salt does not dissolve quickly enough to be used in pastry doughs. As much as you might be tempted to cut down on salt in your cooking,

please use the measure specified in your baking recipes. The flavour of the outcome depends upon it.

SPICES: While I do enjoy the intense flavour of freshly ground spices, I sometimes find that my little grinder can't process them finely enough for delicate desserts (I hate chomping on a big piece of clove or allspice in my dessert). The recipes that appear on these pages are based on the use of store-bought ground spices. The only exception I'll offer is that I prefer to use freshly ground nutmeg, which can be grated with a little nutmeg grater.

Spices do lose their punch after a year (and remember to factor in a few months' shelf time in the store before you buy them), but they don't spoil. I sometimes "up the ante" on the spices I may have had around my kitchen for a while, by adding a dash more than the recipe states.

VANILLA: Only PURE vanilla extract, please. If you are familiar with my baking style, then you know how I love to free-pour vanilla liberally in just about everything. I can be a very cost-conscious person in every other department (and my husband will attest to that), but when it comes to vanilla, there are no substitutes!

When purchasing vanilla beans, look for ones that are pliable and smell strongly when the jar is opened. Since most vanilla beans come sealed, if you arrive home to find your beans brittle and dull, take them back for a refund. Bourbon vanilla is the most common variety, and while Tahitian vanilla has a fatter bean and more floral smell, it has a milder taste.

YEAST: I call for dry active yeast in my recipes because that is what is readily available in grocery stores. If you choose to use instant, otherwise known as quick-dissolve yeast, reduce the measure by one-third and cut your rising time by half. I do find, however convenient, that quick-dissolve yeast doesn't allow for the flavour development that regular yeast does.

Yeast is not nearly as volatile as it once was, so I find that I just give it enough time to dissolve in my liquid, as opposed to waiting for bubbles to start. So long as the expiry date on your package is fine, and you've stored your yeast in a dry, cool place, you should have no troubles.

Tools

BAIN MARIE/WATER BATH: This term refers to placing whatever you are baking in a pan with a lip and filling the pan with boiling water to come halfway up the dessert. This method is the ideal way to cook anything that has a high egg content, as in custards, bread puddings and cheesecakes. The hot water insulates the dessert, so that the centre of the dessert has time to heat up and cook without overcooking the outside.

Admittedly, sometimes I don't feel like putting on the kettle for a couple of cups of water for my cheesecake (unless I'm in the mood for tea). If you have really hot tap water, as I do, that can work just fine.

BAKING PANS: Good quality baking pans are a must for successful desserts. I have gradually accumulated a collection of sizes and shapes over the years that suit all my purposes. Most important are good quality, thick-gauge, baking sheets and good quality springform pans. Springform pans have a hinged ring that clamps onto a base, and the quality of the hinge and seal can mean the difference between a cake in the pan or a cake batter on the bottom of the oven. Removable-bottom tart pans are also useful for attractively presented tarts (and easy removal from the pan).

BENCH/PASTRY SCRAPER: This is my "desert island" baking tool — it's never more than an arm's length away from me in the kitchen. The metal bench scraper is self-explanatory; it is great for scraping up the scraps of dough and flour on your rolling table, but it also doubles as a tool to cut dough and level the sides of a cake. The pastry scraper is a plastic version of this tool with a rounded edge. It is pliable and is perfect for scraping every last bit of batter out of a bowl as well as spreading cake batter into the corners of a square pan and icing cakes, too! It becomes, in effect, an extension of my hand. Look for these tools in a cake supply store or a good kitchen store.

BOWLS: My biggest mistake as a beginner baker was using the wrong-sized bowl for the task. I would end up making an unnecessary mess and twice the number of dirty dishes! Use a big bowl for sifting, whipping and folding things, to give you lots of space to move around. I favour metal bowls over all other varieties, because I can warm them or keep them cold as needed, they don't weigh too much and I can't break them!

COOLING RACK: Placing hot baked goods on a cooling rack allows them to cool properly without the sweating that results in a soggy sweet. A cooling rack should sit at least an inch above the counter to allow good airflow.

ELECTRIC BEATERS/MIXERS: I am hooked on my table-top mixer with its many attachments, but sometimes electric beaters can be more convenient. To really get into making desserts and baking, you will need at least one of these appliances. Again, quality is the key word here — cheaper models have weaker motors that sometimes can't handle heavier doughs or batters.

MEASURES: A good set of measuring cups is indispensable. Be sure to always use dry measuring cups for dry products and liquid measuring cups for liquid products for the most accurate results. The easiest way to measure butter or shortening? The displacement method: to measure $1/2$ cup (125 mL) of butter, fill a liquid measure with cold water to 1 1/2 cups (375 mL) and add butter until the waterline reaches 2 cups (250 mL). Ta-da! That's 1/2 cup (125 mL) of butter!

OVEN: I hear so many people complain about their ovens and it's true, each oven has its own quirks. Get to know your oven — learn where the hot spots are (you know, that place where a cookie always burns, even when all the others are still raw), and keep a thermometer inside to monitor that the temperature is accurate.

When baking, keep the oven door closed as much as possible — an oven loses 25°F (14°C) as soon as you open the door. And as much as I like my convection oven for roasting chicken and potatoes, I keep the fan off for baking. Sugars can brown too quickly in cookies, cakes bake unevenly and custards overcook if the fan is running.

PARCHMENT PAPER: Parchment paper is treated with silicone to keep it from burning as it bakes. I find that using parchment paper extends the life of my baking pans and makes cleaning far easier than when I grease with butter or oil. Parchment paper can be re-used a number of times if it is kept grease-free, as when baking cookies.

PASTRY BRUSH: Pastry brushes come in many widths and are great for brushing syrup or glaze onto cakes and tarts, or for brushing flour off dough or crumbs off a cake. Try to avoid dipping the brush in oil, though (or keep one just for oil), because it will become difficult to clean.

ROLLING PIN: I like to use a wooden rolling pin, but I choose different shapes depending on the task at hand. I like a heavy rolling pin with handles when working with firmer dough, such as puff pastry, but I prefer a smaller pin that is thicker in the middle and thinner at the ends for more delicate pastries and cookies, so I can gently coax the dough into shape.

When rolling, try to always roll from the middle outward and avoid tripping the rolling pin over the edge of the dough. Lift and turn your dough often to make sure it's not sticking to the rolling surface.

ROLLING SURFACE: Many people are surprised to find that I don't use marble for rolling pastry. Marble is a good rolling surface as it stays cool and keeps the dough chilled, but I have grown accustomed over the years to rolling on a wood surface. I find wood maintains an even temperature and, even more important, I find I have less trouble with dough sticking. Using wood, I don't need to add too much flour while rolling dough, so I know my pastries will be tender and won't shrink when baked. A regular formica countertop works fine, just be careful that when you cut your pastry you don't scar your countertop!

SPATULAS: I have three particular spatulas that take care of all my stirring, folding and lifting needs in the kitchen:

Spoonula – This may sound like a ghostly Halloween tool, but it refers to a plastic spatula with a curved bowl surface. It's perfect for scraping every last drop of batter out of a bowl and is ideal for folding in whipped egg whites and creams gently.

Heat-proof spatula – This tool is great for stirring cooking custards and sauces. I used to wreck so many spatulas by accidentally putting them into hot liquids!

Off-set spatula – This is not a stirring tool, but is more used for spreading batters, icing cakes and lifting slices of tart and cake. It comes in different lengths — I favour a 7-inch size for cakes, and a smaller 3-inch one for cookies.

All of these spatulas can be purchased at most kitchen stores, and I've even spotted them at high-end grocery stores.

TIMER: I'd be lost without my kitchen timer. It's bad enough that I have a very poor short-term memory, but when I really get baking and have 4 or 5 things on the go, I rely on my timer to keep me from burning things. I have a magnetic timer that sticks to the oven, but some are made with a clip so you can wear the timer and leave the kitchen to do other tasks.

I always set my timer at least five minutes less than the specified time in a recipe, especially the first time I make something — you just never know!

Techniques

BEAT: To combine vigorously with the goal of quickly bringing ingredients together. By hand, use a quick circular motion, and scrape down the sides of the bowl often. By mixer, use a paddle attachment on medium to medium-high speed.

BLEND: To combine ingredients and achieve an even consistency.

BLIND BAKE: To bake a pie or tart crust by lining with foil and then weighing with pie weights, dried beans or rice. This technique keeps the crust from forming bubbles or air pockets, leaving lots of room for filling.

CREAM: To smooth ingredients together until a creamy consistency is achieved. This term is usually used in reference to combining butter and sugar.

CUT IN: To work cold butter or another fat into a dry mixture without completely blending it in. Use a mixer with the paddle attachment, a pastry cutter (a tool with a number of metal strips), two knives working crosswise, or your fingers. If cutting in butter by hand, work quickly so you don't warm the butter and over-blend it. Little bits of butter should still be visible, and the dough should have a crumbly texture.

DOCK: To mark a dough with a fork to aerate it (just like you should do to your lawn). This allows the dough to remain level, without developing air pockets during baking. The holes give room for the dough to expand as it cooks and, in the case of puff pastry, break a few of the flaky layers to control the height during baking.

FOLD: To gently incorporate an aerated product, such as whipped egg whites or cream, into a heavier base product. Using a spatula or whisk, gently lift the heavier product from the bottom and lift it over the whipped product in a circular motion until it's an even consistency.

As much as it might be tempting to work slowly and deliberately at folding, it is sometimes more effective to work at a moderate speed. The longer you spend folding, the more time the whipped product has to deflate.

GREASE: To evenly coat a pan with fat, such as butter, oil or food release spray. Be certain to get into the corners, as that is where baked goods most often stick. If a recipe calls for greasing and flouring, evenly coat the pan with fat, then sprinkle generously with flour, shaking the pan to get the flour everywhere. Be sure to tap out any excess flour.

SIFT: To pass dry ingredients through a mesh surface to remove naturally occurring lumps. Sifting flour helps ensure a cake will incorporate wet ingredients smoothly and rise evenly during baking.

STIR: To keep ingredients moving by using an even, circular motion. When stirring, be certain the spoon comes in contact with the total surface of the pot or bowl.

fruit

RHUBARB | RASPBERRIES | BLUEBERRIES | CHERRIES | APRICOTS
BLACKBERRIES | NECTARINES | APPLES | GREEN APPLES
CRANBERRIES | CURRANTS | DATES | PINEAPPLES | BANANAS

Rhubarb

For me, rhubarb signals the start of the Canadian fruit season. Once I spot field rhubarb at the farmers' market, I know that the cavalcade of beautiful fruits is soon to follow. While the lovely, feminine pink of hothouse rhubarb requires no treating other than a good wash, the more fibrous field rhubarb benefits from a little peeling. Take a paring knife and pull a little skin away from the stalk and pull down — the peel will release and come away from the stalk when it becomes too thin (and hence tender enough to eat).

Rhubarb Cream Tart

MAKES 1 9-INCH (23-CM) SQUARE FLUTED TART PAN
SERVES 9 TO 12

FRUIT

1 cup	250 mL	sugar
1/3 cup	75 mL	white wine or water
1 tsp	5 mL	vanilla extract
5 cups	1.25 L	chopped fresh rhubarb
1 Tbsp	15 mL	cornstarch
2 Tbsp	25 mL	cold water

CRUST

2 cups	500 mL	graham cracker crumbs
1/4 cup	50 mL	sugar
1/3 cup	75 mL	unsalted butter, melted

MASCARPONE

1/4 cup	50 mL	mascarpone cheese, room temperature
1/4 cup	50 mL	cream cheese, room temperature
3 Tbsp	45 mL	sugar
1 Tbsp	15 mL	grated lemon zest
1 tsp	5 mL	vanilla extract
3/4 cup	175 mL	whipping cream

This tart is really more of a cheesecake. The filling is soft and easy to spread when assembling, but sets up beautifully for clean slices when serving. Try cutting into smaller squares when you need small sweet bites.

FOR FRUIT, preheat oven to 350°F (180°C). Mix sugar, wine and vanilla and toss with rhubarb. Pour into a shallow baking dish and cover. Bake rhubarb for 30 – 40 minutes, until tender.

Strain syrup into a small saucepan, reserving rhubarb. Bring syrup to a simmer. Whisk cornstarch with 2 Tbsp (25 mL) cold water and whisk into liquid, cooking until thickened. Remove from heat and pour over rhubarb. Chill completely.

FOR CRUST, combine graham cracker crumbs and sugar and stir in melted butter until you have an even crumbly texture. Press into a 9-inch (23-cm) square fluted tart pan and bake for 8 minutes. Allow to cool completely.

FOR MASCARPONE, beat both cheeses with electric beaters until smooth and blend in sugar, lemon zest and vanilla. While beating, add whipping cream and mix until thickened, about 2 minutes. Spread filling into crust and top with rhubarb. Chill for at least 2 hours before slicing.

NOTES
❖ Oven poaching the rhubarb ensures that the fruit retains its shape as well as that lovely pink colour.

❖ Try infusing additional flavours into the rhubarb. I favour fresh lavender, lemon zest or even bay leaves.

❖ For a richer tart, replace the cream cheese with an equal amount of mascarpone. For a lighter tart, replace the mascarpone with cream cheese.

Switch Up

Rhubarb Cream Tart with Chocolate Crust

Changing the flavour and appearance of rhubarb dresses up an already delicious crust. Treat the long stalks of cooked rhubarb gently so they don't tear as you remove them from the liquid and arrange them on the tart.

Prepare recipe as on page 23, but substitute 1 dozen stalks of whole fresh rhubarb for diced rhubarb in the fruit. Substitute 2 cups (500 mL) chocolate cookie crumbs for graham crumbs in the crust. To assemble, lay the cooked rhubarb stalks atop the cream for an elegant presentation.

Strawberry Rhubarb Pie

This is my Dad's favourite pie to eat, not just because of the intense springtime combination of strawberries and rhubarb, but because my Mom makes fantastic pies — homemade pies are definitely her strength in the kitchen.

FOR CRUST, combine flour with salt. Cut in butter and shortening until mixture is a roughly even crumbly texture. Add lemon juice and water and blend just until dough comes together. Shape into a disc, wrap and chill for 30 minutes.

Preheat oven to 400°F (200°C). On a lightly floured surface, roll out dough into a circle large enough to fit a 9-inch (23-cm) pie pan. Line pan with pastry, trim and pinch edges. Chill until ready to fill.

FOR FRUIT, toss rhubarb and strawberries with sugar, cornstarch, spices and salt to coat. Fill pie shell with fruit.

FOR CRUMBLE TOPPING, combine flour, sugar, nutmeg and salt. Stir in melted butter just until crumbly and spread over fruit. Bake pie on a tray at 400°F (200°C) for 20 minutes, then reduce heat to 350°F (180°C) and bake for about 40 minutes more, until filling is bubbling.

CRUST

1 1/4 cups	300 mL	all purpose flour
1/4 tsp	1 mL	salt
1/4 cup	50 mL	unsalted butter, chilled
1/4 cup	50 mL	vegetable shortening
1 Tbsp	15 mL	lemon juice
3–5 Tbsp	45–70 mL	cold water

FRUIT

4 cups	1 L	chopped fresh or frozen rhubarb
2 cups	500 mL	strawberries, hulled and sliced
1 cup	250 mL	sugar
3 Tbsp	45 mL	cornstarch
1/2 tsp	2 mL	cinnamon
1/4 tsp	1 mL	ground ginger
		dash salt

CRUMBLE TOPPING

2/3 cup	150 mL	all purpose flour
1/2 cup	125 mL	sugar
1/4 tsp	1 mL	nutmeg
		dash salt
1/4 cup	50 mL	unsalted butter, melted

NOTES

◇ The combination of butter and shortening in the crust makes for a dough that's easier to handle and a little less temperature sensitive than an all-butter crust. Shortening crusts also absorb a little more water than a butter crust, so you may need that full 5 Tbsp (70 mL) measure of water.

◇ The high-temperature oven is needed to kickstart the thickening power of the cornstarch. If your crust begins to brown too quickly, cover the edges with a strip of aluminum foil.

◇ The crumble top to this pie is a good all purpose crumble for coffee cakes and muffins too. Try adding a few chopped pecans or walnuts as an added flavour booster. For a classic double crust pie, double the crust recipe and omit the crumble.

Raspberries

I don't think I've met a single person who didn't like raspberries. My stepdaughter, Mika, and I have gone raspberry picking in the heat of early summer, only to find that we leave the patch with half the berries we picked. Where could they have gone?

Perfect on their own or combined with other flavours, raspberries always add a zip of colour in a dessert. Red raspberries are the best variety to bake with, but the sweeter golden raspberries and intense black raspberries make fantastic garnishes on a dessert plate.

Raspberry Cardamom Cobbler

MAKES 4 INDIVIDUAL COBBLERS OR 1 4-CUP (2-L) BAKING DISH

2 cups	500 mL	red raspberries, fresh or frozen
2 cups	500 mL	Mutsu (Crispin) or Granny Smith apple, peeled and diced
1/2 cup	125 mL	sugar
2 Tbsp	25 mL	all purpose flour
1 tsp	5 mL	cardamom
1/4 tsp	1 mL	cinnamon
2 cups	500 mL	all purpose flour
3 Tbsp	45 mL	cornmeal
2/3 cup	150 mL	sugar
2 tsp	10 mL	baking powder
1/4 tsp	1 mL	salt
2/3 cup	150 mL	unsalted butter, cut into pieces and chilled
2/3 cup	150 mL	milk
1 tsp	5 mL	lemon zest
1 tsp	5 mL	vanilla extract

The hint of lemon and pepper that cardamom adds brings out a floral note in the raspberries. This dessert is just waiting for a big scoop of vanilla ice cream!

If cooking cobbler in a large dish, preheat oven to 325°F (160°C) and if preparing in coffee cups, preheat oven to 350°F (180°C). Toss fruit with 1/2 cup (125 mL) sugar, 2 Tbsp (25 mL) flour, cardamom and cinnamon and spoon into baking dish or ovenproof coffee cups.

In a mixing bowl or in an electric mixer fitted with the paddle attachment, combine remaining flour, cornmeal, 2/3 cup (150 mL) sugar, baking powder and salt. Cut in butter until it's an even crumbly texture. Blend milk, lemon zest and vanilla and add to pastry, mixing until pastry just comes together. Spoon dough onto fruit, leaving a little space between spoonfuls to allow for expansion as cobbler bakes. Bake for 30 – 35 minutes for coffee cups and 45 minutes for large dish.

NOTES

◊ Many coffee cups are ovenproof and so can be used here. I often use previously enjoyed cups (read: garage sale) and mix up the shapes and colours for a funky presentation. Not an occasion for Grandma's fine china!

◊ The focus of flavour in this dessert is definitely on raspberries, but the apple is needed to add body to the cobbler and to absorb all those luscious juices.

◊ If you don't have cardamom, use 1/2 tsp (2 mL) ground black pepper and 1/2 tsp (2 mL) grated lemon zest to replicate the flavour.

Raspberry Cardamom Cobbler with Chantilly Cream, Raspberry Sauce and Maple Toasted Pecans

CHANTILLY CREAM
MAKES 2 CUPS (500 ML)

1 cup	250 mL	whipping cream
2 Tbsp	25 mL	sugar
1 tsp	5 mL	vanilla extract

RASPBERRY SAUCE
MAKES ABOUT 1$\frac{1}{2}$ CUPS (375 ML)

3 cups	750 mL	red raspberries, fresh or frozen
$\frac{2}{3}$ cup	150 mL	sugar
1 tsp	5 mL	lemon zest

MAPLE TOASTED PECANS
MAKES ABOUT 2 CUPS (500 ML)

2 cups	500 mL	pecan halves
3 Tbsp	45 mL	maple syrup

It's amazing how a few added touches can make even the most rustic dessert sparkle!

FOR CREAM, whip cream to soft peaks. Add sugar and vanilla and continue whipping just until cream holds its shape when whisk is lifted.

FOR SAUCE, simmer all ingredients for 10–15 minutes, just enough to melt and incorporate the sugar. Purée and strain. Chill sauce before serving.

FOR PECANS, preheat oven to 350°F (180°C). Toss pecans in maple syrup to coat. Spread pecans out on a parchment-lined baking sheet and toast for 15 minutes, stirring occasionally. Once cooled, the maple syrup will harden onto the nuts.

To assemble, serve cobbler with a dollop of cream and raspberry sauce drizzled over. Nuts can be roughly chopped and scattered on top.

Raspberry Lemon Tart

MAKES 1 10-INCH (25-CM) FLUTED TART PAN
SERVES 10 TO 12

PASTRY

1 cup	250 mL	unsalted butter at room temperature
1/3 cup	75 mL	sugar
4	4	egg yolks
2 cups	500 mL	all purpose flour
1 tsp	5 mL	salt

FILLING

1/3 cup	75 mL	fresh lemon juice
1/4 cup	50 mL	sugar
4	4	eggs
1 cup	250 mL	whipping cream
1 Tbsp	15 mL	lemon zest
4 cups	1 L	fresh raspberries, red, golden, and/or black
		icing sugar, for dusting

NOTES

◇ This pastry recipe likes to be handled. I find I have fewer cracks if I knead the dough a little before rolling.

◇ For ease in filling the tart, place the baked pastry shell on the open oven door, fill and lift into oven (but nine times out of ten, I forget and have to wobble my way across the kitchen).

◇ This tart can be prepared up to a day in advance (but do not cover with plastic wrap — it will stick) and the berries added up to 6 hours ahead of serving.

This tart is a classic French Tarte au Citron, finished with fresh raspberries. I find this dessert most satisfying after a rich meal, such as wintry stew or roast beef. The tartness of the lemon and berries cleanses the palate and a slender slice is not overly filling.

FOR PASTRY, cream butter and sugar together until smooth. Add egg yolks and blend.

Stir in flour and salt and mix just until dough comes together. Turn out onto a lightly floured surface and knead 1 minute. Shape dough into a disc, wrap and chill for at least an hour. If making dough far in advance, remove dough from refrigerator an hour before rolling.

On a lightly floured surface, knead dough again for 1 minute. Roll out pastry to just over 1/4 inch (5 mm) thick. Line a 10-inch (25-cm) removable-bottom tart pan with the dough, trim rough edges and chill for 30 minutes.

Preheat oven to 375°F (190°C). Prick crust bottom with a fork and bake for 15 – 20 minutes, until edges are lightly browned and centre of shell is dry. Allow to cool before filling.

FOR FILLING, reduce oven temperature to 325°F (160°C) and place tart shell on a baking sheet. Whisk together lemon juice, sugar, eggs, cream and zest and pour into tart shell.

Carefully move tart to oven and bake for 25 – 30 minutes, until tart stops jiggling when you tap it. Tart filling should not soufflé at all. Allow tart to cool at room temperature for a bit, then chill for 2 hours before finishing.

To assemble, arrange raspberries on top of tart, starting at the outside edge and moving inwards. Dust lightly with icing sugar if you wish and serve.

Blueberries

My brother's going to roll his eyes at my telling you this, but when he was very little he used to call blueberries "bluebellies" and would hum in his highchair the entire time he was eating a bowl of berries. Admit it — you wish you could do the same without being stared at and whispered about!

Blueberry Buckle

MAKES 1 9-INCH (23-CM) ROUND CAKE
SERVES 10 TO 12

I used to make this coffee cake when I was in university, much to the joy of my housemates. Almost like an upside-down cobbler, this cake satisfies the craving for fruit and cake all at the same time.

FOR CAKE, preheat oven to 350°F (180°C) and grease a 9-inch (23-cm) round cake pan. Cream together butter and sugar until pale yellow. Add egg and vanilla and beat in. Sift together flour, baking powder and salt. Add alternately with milk until incorporated. Scrape batter into cake pan and spread evenly. Sprinkle blueberries on top of batter.

FOR STREUSEL TOPPING, blend sugar, flour and cinnamon in a small bowl. Cut in butter with your fingers until crumbly and no large bits of butter are visible. Sprinkle on top of berries. Bake for 45 – 50 minutes, until a tester inserted in the centre comes out clean of cake (it will have blueberry on it). Allow to cool before slicing.

CAKE

1/2 cup	125 mL	unsalted butter, at room temperature
1/2 cup	125 mL	sugar
1	1	egg
1 tsp	5 mL	vanilla
2 cups	500 mL	all purpose flour
2 1/2 tsp	12 mL	baking powder
1/4 tsp	1 mL	salt
1/2 cup	125 mL	milk
2 cups	500 mL	blueberries, fresh or frozen

STREUSEL TOPPING

1/3 cup	75 mL	sugar
1/3 cup	75 mL	all purpose flour
1/2 tsp	2 mL	cinnamon
3 Tbsp	45 mL	unsalted butter

NOTES

✧ A springform pan for this recipe is great if you wish to present the finished cake at the table. However, if you are just going to portion and serve in the kitchen, baking this in a regular cake pan works just fine.

✧ The dry ingredients of any cake-style method should be sifted to ensure lightness and proper incorporation of the leavenings and salt.

✧ This recipe is also great with raspberries, rhubarb, apple, pear and cranberries or peaches. Try a mix of fruits just for fun.

Blueberry Cream Cheese Cake

CREAM CHEESE FILLING

8 ounces	250 g	cream cheese, at room temperature
1/4 cup	50 mL	sugar
1 tsp	5 mL	vanilla extract
1	1	egg

Adding a cheescake layer to the Blueberry Buckle turns it into a perfect dessert, dressing it up from its coffee cake roots.

Prepare cake and streusel topping as directed on page 29.

FOR CREAM CHEESE FILLING, beat cream cheese in a separate bowl until very smooth. Gradually add sugar, scraping the sides of the mixing bowl well. Add vanilla and blend. Add egg and mix well. Spread cake batter in bottom of prepared pan and spoon cream cheese filling overtop. Top with blueberries and streusel topping. Bake for 50 – 60 minutes, until a tester inserted in the centre of the cake comes out clean of cake. Cool completely before slicing.

Blueberry Ricotta Blintzes

BLINTZ CRÊPES

1 1/4 cups	300 mL	flour
2 Tbsp	25 mL	sugar
4	4	eggs
3/4 cup	175 mL	water
1 1/4 cups	300 mL	milk
1 cup	250 mL	unsalted butter, melted

FILLING

2 cups	500 mL	ricotta cheese
1/4 cup	50 mL	sour cream
1/4 cup	50 mL	sugar
1	1	egg
1	1	egg yolk
1 tsp	5 mL	vanilla extract
		dash nutmeg
2 cups	500 mL	fresh blueberries
		melted butter, for brushing

NOTES

◈ If flipping crêpes presents a challenge, simply turn heat down to medium-low and cook crêpe longer on one side until completely dry-looking (crêpe will cook fully without flipping). Honestly, it took me about 500 crêpes before I really got the hang of it!

◈ It's best not to store crêpes in the fridge — they will dry out. If not using right away, freeze them and thaw when ready to fill. Because of the amount of butter, you do not need to separate each crêpe with waxed paper. Just stack them, cooled, on top of each other and wrap. They will peel away easily once thawed.

These filled crêpes are super tender due to the great amount of butter in them. I do recommend using fresh blueberries, to keep the colour from bleeding through the crêpe and for that "pop" of flavour as you take a bite.

FOR BLINTZ CRÊPES, blend all ingredients with a hand blender (or in a food processor) and let batter rest for 20 minutes. If whisking by hand, strain batter before resting. To make crêpes, heat a large non-stick pan over medium heat. Spray with food release, or lightly coat with oil (you will only have to do this every few crêpes). Pour 1/4 cup (50 mL) of batter into centre of the pan and lift pan off the heat, swirling batter around to coat the pan evenly. Return pan to heat and cook crêpe for 2 – 3 minutes, until edges turn light brown. Gently loosen edges of crêpe with a spatula and flip over in pan. Loosen edges of crêpe and slide onto a plate to cool. Repeat with remaining batter.

After crêpes have cooled, be sure to wrap well until ready to fill.

FOR FILLING, stir together ricotta, sour cream and sugar. Stir in egg, egg yolk, vanilla and nutmeg.

To assemble, preheat oven to 350°F (180°C). Butter a baking pan with melted butter. Place 2 crêpes on work surface, with paler sides facing up. Place about 2 Tbsp (25 mL) fresh blueberries in centre of each crêpe and spoon about 1/4 cup (50 mL) of ricotta filling on top of berries. Fold edges of crêpe over 4 times to create a square parcel. Turn parcel over and place in baking pan. Repeat with remaining crêpes, placing them very close to each other in the pan. Brush tops of blintzes with butter, and sprinkle with a little sugar. Bake for 15 – 20 minutes, until they puff up like little pillows. Serve immediately, dusted generously with icing sugar and with a little blueberry sauce or fresh berries. A scoop of vanilla ice cream also has a place on such a dessert!

Cherries

"Sweet and sour" takes on a different meaning when talking about cherries. Dark, plump, sweet cherries are harvested weeks in advance of sour or tart cherries, which have that vibrant bright red colour that matches their tart personality.

I have the good fortune to live near the heart of Ontario's tender fruit belt, which includes cherry orchards. What a joy it is to drive through the winding roads of Niagara to catch sight of the pink and white blossoms. The challenge is having the patience to wait for the fruits that follow two months after the flowers!

One Step Cherry Pie

MAKES 1 9-INCH (23-CM) PIE
SERVES 6 TO 8

2 cups	500 mL	sweet cherries
1 Tbsp	15 mL	unsalted butter
1 cup	250 mL	all purpose flour
1/4 tsp	1 mL	cinnamon
		dash salt
5	5	eggs
5 Tbsp	70 mL	sugar
1 cup	250 mL	milk
		icing sugar, for dusting

This recipe is essentially a French clafouti. The texture is a cross between a crêpe and a cake and traditionally is made with unpitted cherries (but I find pitting the cherries worth the end result). This recipe comes together so effortlessly, I've made it for many Olson family gatherings when I need to put together a nice dessert in a hurry.

Preheat oven to 350°F (180°C). Pit cherries and set aside. Rub a pie dish or round baking dish with 1 Tbsp (15 mL) unsalted butter. Sift flour with cinnamon and salt into a medium bowl. Add eggs, sugar and milk and whisk together (will be the consistency of crêpe batter). Pour into baking dish and sprinkle cherries over. Bake for 30 minutes, until set.

Dust generously with icing sugar and serve immediately.

NOTES

❀ Most cherry desserts call for sour cherries. The subtly sweet cherries make a delicious change here.

❀ A cherry pitter is a smart and reasonable investment to make (it works well for pitting olives too), but be sure to wear an apron or a red top while pitting your cherries!

❀ This recipe translates wonderfully into a winter dessert by using dried cherries, dried cranberries or currants.

[Switch Up]

Cherry Tarts with Sugared Almonds   MAKES 6 4-INCH (10-CM) INDIVIDUAL TARTS

KIRSCH GLAZE

2 Tbsp	25 mL	kirsch liqueur
6 Tbsp	90 mL	icing sugar
1 Tbsp	15 mL	milk

SUGARED ALMONDS

1 Tbsp	15 mL	egg white
2 Tbsp	25 mL	sugar
2 cups	500 mL	sliced almonds

Individualizing this dessert and glazing the tarts is a great way to dress it up and make each guest at your next dinner party feel special. The added touch of a sugared almond garnish just adds a little more sparkle.

Prepare One Step Cherry Pie, page 32, and fill 6 buttered 4-inch (10-cm) tart shells and bake for 20–25 minutes.

FOR KIRSCH GLAZE, whisk ingredients together and brush over tarts while still warm.

FOR SUGARED ALMONDS, preheat oven to 350°F (180°C). Whisk egg white until foamy. Add sugar and whisk until white, but not meringue-like. Fold in almonds to coat. Spoon almonds onto a parchment-lined baking sheet and bake for 15 minutes, stirring occasionally. Allow to cool before using. To serve, scatter sugared almonds over finished tarts.

Black Forest Molten Cake

CHERRY FILLING

1 cup	250 mL	pitted sour cherries
1/2 cup	125 mL	sugar

BRANDIED CHERRY SAUCE

2 cups	500 mL	sweet cherries, pitted
1/2 cup	125 mL	sugar
1	1	cinnamon stick
1/4 cup	50 mL	brandy
4 1/2 tsp	18 mL	cornstarch
2 Tbsp	25 mL	cold water

CAKE

8 ounces	250 g	bittersweet chocolate, chopped
1/2 cup	125 mL	unsalted butter, plus enough for greasing ramekins
2/3 cup	150 mL	sugar, plus enough for coating ramekins
3	3	eggs, at room temperature
1 tsp	5 mL	vanilla
1/4 cup	50 mL	all purpose flour
1/4 cup	50 mL	cocoa powder
		dash salt

NOTES

❖ When cooking sour cherries, don't be surprised if the colour blanches out initially. Just keep simmering them and the colour will return.

❖ I find the intensity of bittersweet chocolate grabs you in this recipe more than semisweet chocolate might, especially as it's served warm.

❖ Try a few fresh raspberries in the centre of the cakes in place of cherries. Or how about a soft caramel candy or two?

Ordering one black forest cake, hold the cream and double the chocolate! This is the dessert that has replaced crème brûlée as the top-seller on most restaurant dessert menus. When preparing these at home, put the cakes in the oven right when you're finishing your main course and within minutes the house will start filling with the scent of chocolate, reminding your guests that they have just a little more room than they thought for dessert!

FOR CHERRY FILLING, simmer cherries with 1/2 cup (125 mL) sugar for 30 minutes and allow to cool.

FOR BRANDIED CHERRY SAUCE, simmer cherries, sugar and cinnamon for 30 minutes. Stir in brandy. Whisk cornstarch with cold water and whisk into cherries. Be certain that cherries are simmering before you remove from heat. Serve sauce warm or chilled.

FOR CAKE, preheat oven to 375°F (190°C). Butter 6 5-ounce (150-mL) ramekins and coat with sugar. Melt chocolate over a pot of simmering water (or in microwave), stirring often, and remove from heat. In a separate bowl cream together butter and 2/3 cup (150 mL) sugar. Add eggs one at a time, mixing well after each addition. Stir in melted chocolate and vanilla. In a separate bowl, sift together flour, cocoa powder and salt. Stir flour mixture into chocolate mixture. Spoon batter evenly into ramekins. Place a generous spoonful of cherries in the centre of each ramekin and level chocolate filling to create a flat surface. Bake for 20 – 22 minutes. The surfaces of the cakes will lose their shine when done. The batter can be made ahead of time and chilled, but add 10 minutes to the cooking time.

To serve, run a butter knife around the edge of the cake to loosen and tip out onto plate and serve with brandied cherry sauce.

Apricots

Apricots might very well be the pastry chef's favourite fruit. They retain their colour when cooked, they improve in flavour when baked, they hold their shape and they don't make cakes or tarts watery as they bake. Absolutely perfect.

Vanilla Roasted Apricots

SERVES 6

12	12	fresh apricots
3 Tbsp	45 mL	unsalted butter, melted
2 Tbsp + 1/4 cup	25 mL + 50 mL	sugar
1/4 cup	50 mL	honey
2 Tbsp	25 mL	lemon juice
2	2	vanilla beans

The satisfying scent of apricots roasting with vanilla is just so enticing! Pour table cream over top for an added treat.

Preheat oven to 375°F (190°C). Wash, halve and pit apricots. Toss with melted butter and add 2 Tbsp (25 mL) sugar. Toss well so that the sugar sticks to the buttered apricots. Pour into a baking dish.

In a small saucepan, blend remaining 1/4 cup (50 mL) sugar, honey and lemon juice. Scrape the seeds from the vanilla beans into the pan and add the pods for extra flavour. Heat on medium just until sugar dissolves. Pour over apricots and roast, uncovered, for 20 – 25 minutes. While roasting, baste apricots with syrup, but agitate fruit as little as possible. Spoon into bowls and serve warm.

NOTES

⬦ Eliminate the step of coating the apricots with butter and sugar and serve the apricots alone for a completely fat-free dessert.

⬦ Try serving the apricots on the side of a rich chocolate dessert or with a custard dessert, such as crème brûlée.

⬦ Puréeing the roasted apricots and their juices produces an intensely flavoured sauce to serve with ice cream or a fruit tart.

Vanilla Apricots with Brown Sugar Shortbread and Skyr

SHORTBREAD

1 cup	250 mL	unsalted butter, at room temperature
1 cup	250 mL	light brown sugar, packed
1 tsp	5 mL	vanilla extract
2¼ cups	550 mL	all purpose flour, sifted
		dash salt

SKYR
MAKES ABOUT 1¾ CUPS (425 ML)

3 cups	750 mL	full fat yoghurt, without gelatin or cornstarch listed on ingredients
2 Tbsp	25 mL	honey

The addition of brown sugar shortbread to this dessert gives you something to soak up those lovely, perfumey juices at the bottom of your bowl. "Skyr" is the Icelandic term for strained yoghurt and makes a great, light, creamy topping.

FOR SHORTBREAD, preheat oven to 325°F (160°C). Cream together butter, sugar and vanilla until light and fluffy. Stir in flour and salt until dough comes together. Scrape dough into a greased 9-inch (23-cm) square or round pan and press in. Chill for 20 minutes.

Dock shortbread with a fork and bake for 25–30 minutes, just until edges have browned a little. It is easiest to cut shortbread while it's warm.

FOR SKYR, prepare a day ahead. Spoon yoghurt into a cheesecloth-lined strainer and let drain in the fridge (over a bowl) overnight. The next day, remove the yoghurt from the strainer and blend in honey.

To serve, spoon a nice dollop of skyr over warm apricots with a couple of slices of brown sugar shortbread tucked just inside the bowl.

Apricot Linzer Torte

FILLING

2 cups	500 mL	fresh apricots, washed and pitted
2/3 cup	150 mL	apricot jam
1/4 cup	50 mL	sugar
		zest of one orange

LINZER DOUGH

3	3	hard-boiled eggs
1 1/4 cups	300 mL	unsalted butter, at room temperature
1/2 cup	125 mL	icing sugar
		dash vanilla extract
1 1/2 tsp	7 mL	rum
1/2 cup	125 mL	ground hazelnuts, lightly toasted
3/4 tsp	4 mL	salt
1/4 tsp	1 mL	baking powder
2 1/4 cups	550 mL	all purpose flour

1 egg, mixed with 2 Tbsp (25 mL) cold water

The traditional Austrian Linzer Torte is made with an almond pastry and filled with raspberry jam. I have taken shameless but satisfying liberties with this classic by using a hazelnut dough with an apricot filling.

Also traditional is a woven lattice-top to this torte. To make life easier, I use small cookie cutters and punch out holes in the top layer of dough. This way I can see the bright fruit filling, and avoid giving myself a headache by weaving the pastry.

FOR FILLING, simmer all ingredients in a big saucepan until apricots are tender. Remove from heat, purée and cool completely before using.

FOR LINZER DOUGH, peel hard-boiled eggs and remove whites. Push yolks through a sieve and set aside.

Cream together butter and icing sugar until smooth. Stir in vanilla extract and rum. Blend in hazelnuts and cooked egg yolks. Sift salt, baking powder and flour and add to butter mixture. Blend until dough comes together (it will be quite soft). Divide dough into 2 discs, wrap and chill for 1 1/2 hours, until firm.

Preheat oven to 350°F (180°C). On a lightly floured surface, roll one disc of dough to 1/2 inch (1 cm) thick. Using the bottom of a 10-inch (25-cm) removable-bottom tart pan as your template, cut out a disc of pastry. Repeat with the second disc of pastry.

Using the tart pan bottom as a lifter, transfer the first disc of pastry to a parchment-lined baking sheet. Spread the apricot filling over the entire surface of the dough. If the dough is very soft, I like to flash it in the freezer for 5 minutes, to make spreading the filling easier.

(CONTINUES NEXT PAGE)

NOTES

✧ It is the hard-boiled egg yolk that gives this dough its distinct tenderness. Use the remaining cooked whites chopped up in a salad (then you earn the right to have a second slice of dessert).

✧ I choose to use the reverse side of a round pastry tip as my cutter. You could easily use a small heart-shaped or star-shaped cutter and create your own look.

✧ This dough freezes very well. Thaw in the fridge for a few hours, then knead just a moment to make it easy to roll.

Using a $3/4$-inch (2-cm) round cutter (I actually use the bottom of a large piping tip), cut 8 holes around the second disc. Punch a hole at 12 o'clock, then at 6, 9 and 3 o'clock and fill in with holes between those spaces. Following the line of these holes, use a $1/4$-inch (5-mm) cutter (or smaller pastry tip) and punch smaller holes closer to the centre of the torte.

While it's still on the cutting board, brush the top of the disc generously with egg wash. Place gently on top of apricot filling. Place ring of a springform pan around torte to help it hold shape while cooking. Bake for 35 – 40 minutes, until it's a rich golden brown. Allow to cool before cutting.

Linzer Torte is best served at room temperature, but can be stored for 2 – 3 days refrigerated.

Blackberries

Blackberries have the full season of summer to grow and ripen, and I find when you pop one in your mouth it's a gushing cool drink of water. At the restaurant, I had a blackberry supplier, Bob, who would grow the best fruit during his summers off as a school teacher.

Blackberry Frozen Yoghurt

MAKES ABOUT 4 CUPS (1 L)
SERVES 4 TO 6

5 cups	1.25 L	blackberries, fresh or frozen
1/2 cup	125 mL	superfine sugar (fruit sugar)
2 Tbsp	25 mL	water
1 tsp	5 mL	lime zest
1 1/2 cups	375 mL	yoghurt
1/2 cup	125 mL	whipping cream

This frozen yoghurt almost qualifies as a sorbet, it is so packed with fruit.

Crush blackberries (or purée) and press through a fine strainer. Stir in sugar, water and lime zest and let sit, covered, for about 30 minutes, until sugar is dissolved. Stir in yoghurt. Whip cream to soft peaks and fold in.

Freeze yoghurt in ice cream maker following manufacturer's instructions. Frozen yoghurt is delicious if served while it's still soft or you can scrape it into a container and freeze until firm.

NOTES

❖ When buying blackberries, look for evenly coloured berries without any paler spots. They will be sweeter.

❖ Using low fat yoghurt is just fine in this recipe.

❖ Crushing the berries without cooking them in this recipe ensures an exceptionally fresh taste.

Blackberry Frozen Yoghurt in Lime Cups

For a more dramatic presentation, serve this frozen yoghurt in lime cups. The contrast of the rich blackberry colour against the lime green looks as good as it tastes.

Prepare 6 limes by cutting off the top third. Thinly slice the bottom of each lime so that it sits level. Hollow out lime. Scoop or pipe Blackberry Frozen Yoghurt into lime and freeze for approximately 1 hour. Serve frozen.

Pineapple Carrot Mini Cakes 62

Blackberry Steamed Puddings

PUDDINGS

2 cups	500 mL	blackberries, fresh or frozen, if using ramekins — OR 1 cup (250 mL) if using baba tins
3	3	eggs, separated
1/2 cup	125 mL	sugar, plus additional for coating ramekins
1	1	vanilla bean
1 Tbsp	25 mL	lemon zest
2 tsp	10 mL	unsalted butter, melted
2/3 cup	150 mL	buttermilk, room temperature
1 3/4 cups	425 mL	all purpose flour
1 tsp	5 mL	baking powder
1/2 tsp	2 mL	cinnamon
		dash salt

ORANGE BUTTERMILK SAUCE

1/3 cup	75 mL	sugar
1 Tbsp	15 mL	cornstarch
3 Tbsp	45 mL	orange juice (freshly squeezed)
1 Tbsp	15 mL	lemon juice
2/3 cup	150 mL	buttermilk
1	1	egg yolk
1 Tbsp	15 mL	orange zest
1 tsp	5 mL	unsalted butter

Don't expect a pudding by North American standards. This is not a chilled custard dessert, but a light steamed cake that, when inverted, has a thick layer of juicy blackberries to create a built-in syrup. Served with an orange buttermilk sauce, it is really an elegant ending to a meal.

FOR PUDDINGS, preheat oven to 375°F (190°C). Grease 6 5-ounce (150-mL) ramekins or baba tins and coat with sugar, shaking off excess. Distribute blackberries among ramekins and place in a baking dish with at least a 2-inch (5-cm) lip.

Whisk by hand the egg yolks, sugar, and scraped seeds from vanilla bean until pale and thick. Whisk in lemon zest, butter and buttermilk. In a separate bowl, sift together dry ingredients (except for salt) and whisk into buttermilk mixture. Whip egg whites and salt to stiff peaks and fold in one-third, then remaining two-thirds of whites. Spoon into ramekins and place ramekins in a baking pan. Pour boiling water halfway up outsides of ramekins. Cover pan with plastic wrap, then foil and bake for 35 – 40 minutes (until cake springs back when touched). Carefully remove foil and plastic and take ramekins out of water bath. Let cool for 5 minutes.

FOR ORANGE BUTTERMILK SAUCE, combine all ingredients except butter in a saucepan. Stir with a wooden spoon over medium heat until sauce coats the back of a spoon, about 4 minutes. Strain and stir in butter. Chill until ready to serve.

To serve, pool some Orange Buttermilk Sauce in the bottom of a flat-bottomed bowl or onto a plate. Invert a warm pudding over sauce, so that berries are on top.

NOTES

⟡ The sugar on the sides of the ramekins allow the cake to "climb" as it rises and hold in the air for a light, fluffy texture.

⟡ These are, of course, just as delicious with raspberries or apple slices at the bottom of each ramekin in place of blackberries.

⟡ If you have baba tins, use them for this dessert. You get a fabulously tall individual cake to present to your guests.

Nectarines

Named for its sweet nectar, nectarines follow peaches by season, as they need just that little bit of extra sunshine to ripen them. My personal choice in using nectarines over peaches comes from the fact that you don't need to peel them. The thin, tender skin melts away in your mouth as easily as the juicy flesh.

Nectarine Raspberry Turnovers   MAKES 12 TURNOVERS

4	4	nectarines, diced (not peeled)
1 1/2 cups	375 mL	raspberries, fresh or frozen (be certain to drain frozen well)
1/4 cup	50 mL	sugar
3 Tbsp	45 mL	all purpose flour
1/2 tsp	2 mL	cinnamon
1/4 tsp	1 mL	nutmeg
6	6	sheets phyllo pastry
2/3 cup	150 mL	unsalted butter, melted
		turbinado sugar, for sprinkling

These are a dessert version of spanakopita. A great pick-up-and-go treat, these would be perfect packed in a lunch or taken on a picnic.

Preheat oven to 350°F (180°C). Toss diced nectarines with raspberries, sugar, flour, cinnamon and nutmeg and set aside. Lay out 1 sheet of phyllo pastry on work surface (keep unused phyllo under a moist towel to prevent drying). Brush sheet with butter and lay a second sheet of phyllo on top. Brush with butter, lay a third sheet of phyllo over and brush with butter. Cut phyllo into 6 equal lengths, with cuts starting from the long side. Place a generous spoonful of filling at one end of a strip. Fold up one corner edge of pastry strip so it makes a triangle over fruit. Fold pastry over again, building on the triangle shape. Keep folding until all pastry has been folded over fruit, trimming off excess. Place on a parchment-lined baking sheet. Repeat with remaining 5 strips and start entire process again with remaining 3 sheets of phyllo pastry.

Brush turnovers with melted butter and sprinkle with turbinado sugar. Bake for 20 – 30 minutes, until a light golden brown. Enjoy warm or at room temperature.

Turnovers will keep refrigerated for 2 – 3 days, but warm in oven or microwave to serve.

Nectarine Raspberry Strudel

MAKES 1 STRUDEL
SERVES 10

The same flavour combination as the turnovers gets dressed up as a strudel to be sliced and served to guests.

Build the filling (see page 42), and layer all 6 sheets of phyllo on top of each other, each lightly brushed with melted butter. Spoon nectarine filling along long end of pastry, leaving 2 inches (5 cm) at either end. Roll up phyllo, encompassing fruit. After first roll that covers fruit, fold over outside edges to seal in ends of strudel and continue rolling (like making a giant burrito). Lift carefully and place seam-side-down onto a parchment-lined baking sheet.

Brush strudel with butter and sprinkle with turbinado sugar. Pierce top of strudel to allow steam to escape. Bake for 25 – 35 minutes, until strudel is a light golden brown. Enjoy warm or at room temperature.

Strudel will keep 2 – 3 days refrigerated; simply warm in oven or microwave to serve.

NOTES

❖ Try using puff pastry instead of phyllo, for a switch. Roll out dough to $^1/4$-inch (5-mm) thickness, cut in squares, fill and fold over to make triangles.

❖ Nectarines bruise easily, so treat them gently. If there is any bruising, trim it away.

❖ To test the ripeness of a nectarine, sniff it at the stem end. If you can pick up the faint scent of flowers, then it's ready to eat!

Nectarine Flan

CAKE

3	3	eggs
1/2 cup	125 mL	sugar
1/3 cup	75 mL	all purpose flour
4 1/2 tsp	18 mL	cornstarch
1/4 tsp	1 mL	baking powder
1/4 tsp	1 mL	salt
1/4 cup	50 mL	unsalted butter, melted
1/2 tsp	2 mL	vanilla extract

SYRUP

1/4 cup	50 mL	sugar
1/4 cup	50 mL	water
1 Tbsp	15 mL	lemon juice

FILLING

2/3 cup	150 mL	sugar
1/4 cup	50 mL	cornstarch
1 1/2 cups	375 mL	buttermilk
6 Tbsp	90 mL	lemon juice
1	1	egg yolk
1 Tbsp	15 mL	unsalted butter
1 tsp	5 mL	lemon zest
5 – 6	5 – 6	nectarines, sliced
1 cup	250 mL	raspberries or blueberries
1/4 cup	50 mL	clear apricot jam or apple jelly

Cake, custard and fruit — what a combination! I use a lemon buttermilk custard filling that's tart and refreshing and a good contrast to sweet summer fruits.

FOR CAKE, preheat oven to 350°F (180°C). Prepare 9-inch (23-cm) springform pan by greasing and coating with sugar, shaking out excess. In a metal bowl over a pot of gently simmering water, whisk eggs and sugar together until warm. Pour into a mixer fitted with the whisk attachment, or whip with electric beaters, until batter is thick and holds a ribbon when whisk is lifted. Sift together flour, cornstarch, baking powder and salt, and with mixer on medium, add flour all at once and mix just until blended. Combine melted butter and vanilla, add all at once and blend. Scrape batter into prepared pan and bake for 18 – 20 minutes, until cake springs back when gently pressed. Allow to cool, then remove from pan.

FOR SYRUP, simmer sugar, water and lemon juice for 5 minutes, then remove from heat and cool.

FOR FILLING, combine sugar and cornstarch in a saucepan. Whisk in buttermilk and lemon juice. Whisk in egg yolk. Bring to a simmer over medium heat, stirring until thickened, 7 – 9 minutes. Remove from heat, strain and stir in butter and lemon zest. Cover surface of filling with plastic wrap and chill completely before using. Filling will thicken more as it cools.

To assemble, brush flan cake with syrup. Whisk filling to smooth out, then spread over flan. Arrange nectarine slices over filling and dot with berries. Melt jam or jelly in microwave (or in a saucepan over low heat) and brush over fruit to make it glisten.

NOTES

⬦ Nectarines don't oxidize (turn brown) as quickly as peaches, so they're a great topper for any cake.

⬦ Something to consider — the lemon buttermilk filling only has 1 Tbsp (15 mL) butter and 1 egg yolk. Quite low in fat, really, but you'd never guess by tasting it!

⬦ The separate components of this flan can be made up to 2 days ahead, but assembled the day you plan on serving it.

Apples

I always have a few apples in my crisper, so I often have reason to make an apple dessert. There's something utterly wholesome about apple desserts — you feel like you're indulging in something nutritious.

I favour Mutsu apples, sometimes known as Crispin, as they are available from mid-October through to March. They have a good balance of acidity and sweetness and they hold their shape when cooked. If that's not an option, try a Granny Smith, Spartan or Spy.

Apple Date Cheddar Muffins

MAKES 6 JUMBO OR 12 REGULAR MUFFINS

1	1	egg
1/4 cup	50 mL	vegetable oil
1 cup	250 mL	milk
1 cup	250 mL	sugar
1 cup	250 mL	all purpose flour
1 cup	250 mL	whole wheat flour
1 Tbsp	15 mL	baking powder
1/2 tsp	2 mL	salt
1 cup +2 Tbsp	250 mL + 25 mL	grated cheddar cheese
1 cup	250 mL	Mutsu or Granny Smith apples, peeled and diced
1/2 cup	125 mL	dates, chopped
2 Tbsp	25 mL	dark brown sugar, packed

Snack? Breakfast? Dessert? These are definitely an anytime sweet treat.

Preheat oven to 350°F (180°C). Grease a jumbo 6-muffin tin (or a regular 12-muffin tin). Whisk together egg, oil, milk and sugar. In a separate bowl, sift flours, baking powder and salt and stir into egg mixture. Fold in 1 cup (250 mL) cheese, apples and dates. Bake for 30 minutes. Combine remaining 2 Tbsp (15 mL) cheddar with brown sugar and sprinkle on top of muffins for the last 10 minutes of baking. Enjoy warm with sweet butter.

NOTES

✧ Use any type of cheddar you like — I favour medium. White or orange makes no difference.

✧ I find the combination of whole wheat flour and dates creates the effect of sticky toffee pudding. These muffins are always moist.

✧ The best way to refresh a stale muffin is to brush it with a little milk and warm it in a 300°F (180°C) oven for a few minutes. Just like freshly baked!

Apple Cheddar Loaf with Walnut Hard Sauce

MAKES 1 9 x 5-INCH (2-L) LOAF
SERVES 10 TO 12

WALNUT HARD SAUCE
MAKES ABOUT 2 CUPS (500 ML)

½ cup	125 mL	unsalted butter
1 cup	250 mL	dark brown sugar, packed
1 tsp	5 mL	cinnamon
¼ cup	50 mL	whiskey or brandy
½ cup	125 mL	whipping cream
1 cup	250 mL	walnut pieces, lightly toasted

Serving this loaf with a dessert sauce is perfect if you're having the girls over for a game of cards!

Make the Apple Date Cheddar Muffin recipe (see page 45) but bake it in a greased 9 x 5-inch (2-L) loaf pan for 40 minutes, until a tester inserted in the centre of the loaf comes out clean (and add the cheddar sprinkle during the last 10 minutes of baking).

FOR WALNUT HARD SAUCE, melt butter with brown sugar over medium-high heat. Stir in cinnamon. Bring up to a simmer, stirring. Add whiskey carefully (watching for flames). Stir in cream and simmer for 1 minute. Remove from heat and stir in walnuts. Sauce can be chilled and reheated in the microwave.

To serve, spoon warm sauce over slices of apple loaf.

Alsatian Apple Tart

SABLÉ CRUST

1 1/4 cups	300 mL	pastry flour
1 cup	250 mL	icing sugar
1/4 tsp	1 mL	salt
1/2 cup + 2 Tbsp	125 mL + 25 mL	unsalted butter, cut into pieces and chilled
3	3	egg yolks

FILLING

1/3 cup	75 mL	sour cream
3 Tbsp	45 mL	sugar
		dash nutmeg
8	8	Granny Smith apples
2 Tbsp	25 mL	lemon juice
2 Tbsp	25 mL	Calvados or brandy
3 Tbsp	45 mL	apricot or apple jelly

Stacked high with slender apple slices, this tart is definitely a showpiece. The crust is a sweet dough, making for a tender, truly succulent dessert.

FOR SABLÉ CRUST, sift together flour, icing sugar and salt. Cut in butter until the pastry starts to take on a yellow colour. Mix in yolks until dough is an even texture. Shape into a disc, wrap and chill for 1 hour.

Preheat oven to 350°F (180°C). On a lightly floured surface, roll out dough to just greater than 1/4 inch (5 mm) thick. Line a 10-inch (25-cm) removable-bottom tart pan with pastry and trim edges. Chill for 15 minutes. Dock with a fork and bake for 18–20 minutes until it just begins to brown at edges. Allow to cool.

FOR FILLING, blend sour cream, sugar and nutmeg and spread over bottom of cooled crust. Peel and core apples, and thinly slice with a mandolin (or slice as thinly as possible by hand). Sprinkle apples with lemon juice and Calvados. Line tart shell with apple slices, starting at the outside and overlapping slices 3/4 over each other. Spiral apple slices toward the centre, creating a tart that is taller in the centre than at the edge. Bake for 25–30 minutes, until apples are tender. Warm jelly with a tablespoon (15 mL) of water and brush over tart to glaze. Chill until ready to serve.

NOTES

◇ Sablé means "sand" in French, and this crust has a very fine texture to it. In fact, this recipe works well for cut-out cookies, and the dough also freezes well.

◇ Test the doneness of the apples by inserting a skewer. If it slides in without resistance, then the apples are cooked.

◇ Glazing the tart with jelly adds sweetness, shine and keeps the air out, preventing discolouration.

Green Apples

Why devote a number of recipes to just green apples? Available virtually year round, they never fail to be tart, exceptionally juicy and flavourful. For this they can be relied upon as a key ingredient in successful desserts. How about them apples?

Green Apple Bread Pudding

MAKES 1 9-INCH (23-CM) SQUARE BAKING DISH
SERVES 6 TO 9

5 Tbsp	70 mL	unsalted butter, melted
1/2	1/2	large baguette, cubed
1 cup	250 mL	green apple, peeled and cubed
3 Tbsp	45 mL	raisins
2	2	egg yolks
2	2	whole eggs
1/3 cup	75 mL	sugar
1 1/4 cups	300 mL	whipping cream
1 cup	250 mL	milk
2 tsp	10 mL	vanilla extract
1/4 cup	50 mL	Irish cream (optional)
		sugar for sprinkling
		maple syrup for brushing

Just when I think I have nothing in my pantry to turn into a dessert, my eyes will fall upon that leftover baguette that has seen fresher days. In minutes, the custard base is mixed and soon after I'm enjoying the homey taste of one of my favourite comfort foods, with the final glaze of maple syrup as the perfect finishing touch.

Preheat oven to 350°F (180°C). Butter the sides of a 9-inch (23-cm) square baking dish and use the remaining butter to spread on the bread. Toss bread cubes, apples and raisins together with melted butter and pour into the baking dish.

Whisk together egg yolks, whole eggs and sugar. Whisk in cream, milk and vanilla. Pour over bread cubes and press down gently on bread to help liquid soak in. Let stand for about 15 minutes. If you wish, drizzle with Irish cream.

Place baking dish into a larger pan and pour boiling water around pudding dish, halfway up sides. Sprinkle top of pudding with sugar. Bake for 50 – 60 minutes, until the centre of the pudding springs back when pressed. Remove baking dish from water bath. Brush maple syrup over surface of pudding and serve warm.

NOTES

✤ Substitute the raisins with dried cranberries, dried cherries or walnuts for variety.

✤ For added richness, raisin bread or egg bread (even brioche) instead of baguette would be a hit.

✤ Use half-and-half cream in place of whipping cream for a lighter bread pudding. Then you could get away with eating it for breakfast!

✤ This ratio of eggs, milk and cream is known as a "royale" and is the base for other dishes such as quiches and stratas (a savoury bread pudding).

Bread Pudding with Calvados Anglaise

CALVADOS ANGLAISE

MAKES ABOUT 1⅓ CUPS (325 ML)

I cup	250 mL	half-and-half cream
I tsp	5 mL	vanilla extract
2	2	egg yolks
¼ cup	50 mL	sugar
4½ tsp	22 mL	Calvados

Calvados is a French apple brandy that ties the sauce to the sweetness of apples in the pudding. If Calvados is unavailable, regular brandy or rum will add that needed "kick."

Bring cream with vanilla up to just below a simmer. Whisk together egg yolks and sugar until pale. Gently whisk cream into egg mixture and return to pot. With a wooden spoon over medium-low heat, stir sauce until it coats the back of a spoon, about 4 minutes. Strain and stir in Calvados. Allow to cool.

To serve, cut a square of warm bread pudding and place in a bowl. Drizzle cooled custard sauce over and serve.

Deep Dish Apple Pie

PASTRY

2 cups	500 mL	all purpose flour
2 Tbsp	25 mL	sugar
1/2 tsp	2 mL	baking powder
1/2 tsp	2 mL	salt
1/2 cup	125 mL	unsalted butter, cut into pieces and chilled
1	1	egg
3–4 Tbsp	45–60 mL	milk

APPLES

8	8	large Granny Smith apples, peeled, cored and sliced
2 cups	500 mL	water
2	2	strips orange zest
6	6	whole cloves
2	2	cinnamon sticks
1/2 tsp	2 mL	ground nutmeg
3/4 cup	175 mL	sugar

1 egg mixed with 2 Tbsp (25 mL) milk for glazing

A pie built for the ultimate apple-pie lover. Baked in a springform pan, this pie presents beautifully, and when sliced reveals a dense apple filling with no air pockets or room for anything but your fork.

FOR PASTRY, combine flour, sugar, baking powder and salt. Cut in butter until pastry is an even, crumbly texture. Whisk together egg and 3 Tbsp (45 mL) milk. Add to dough and mix until dough comes together, adding additional milk if needed. Shape dough into a disc, wrap and chill for 30 minutes.

FOR APPLES, bring apples up to a simmer with water, orange zest, cloves, cinnamon, nutmeg and sugar. Simmer for 15 minutes, until apples are tender. Drain and remove zest, cloves and cinnamon. Allow to cool to room temperature.

Preheat oven to 350°F (180°C). Roll out two-thirds of pastry to just less than 1/4 inch (5 mm) thick on a lightly floured surface. Line an 8-inch (20-cm) springform pan carefully, letting pastry hang a little over the sides. Roll out remaining one-third of dough large enough to cover top of pan. Fill pan with apples and brush edges of pastry with egg wash. Place disc of pastry over fruit and seal edge, trim and crimp. Make holes in pastry with a fork or scissors and brush with remaining egg wash. Bake for 55 – 65 minutes, until pastry is a rich golden brown. Let pie rest for 20 minutes before removing springform ring.

NOTES

✧ Don't have time to make scratch dough? Use store-bought puff pastry for fast results.

✧ Cooking the apples a little before they go into the pie allows them to hold their shape and colour, keep in all their yummy juices and absorb subtle flavours.

✧ Crimping the edges of a pie just takes a little practice. Treat your pastry like modeling clay — if you're not happy with your "work of art," just re-shape the dough and start again.

Cranberries

Cranberries represent the epitome of autumn fruits, and I would almost call them our northern citrus fruit — they add tartness to any dish, are incredibly high in vitamin C and they make great juice. In baking, I like to use both fresh and frozen cranberries (they do freeze so well) to heighten other less acidic fruits such as pears and apricots.

Cranberry Gratin

MAKES 1 6-CUP (1.5-L) DISH
SERVES 6 TO 8

4 cups	1 L	fresh or frozen cranberries
1/2 cup	125 mL	whipping cream
1/2 cup	125 mL	dry breadcrumbs
1 cup	250 mL	ground almonds
2	2	eggs
3/4 cup	175 mL	sugar
1 tsp	5 mL	lime zest
1 tsp	5 mL	vanilla extract
1/2 tsp	2 mL	almond extract
		icing sugar, for dusting

Call it a slump or a grunt, this dessert is simple to make and even more gratifying to eat.

Preheat oven to 400°F (200°C). Pour cranberries into a 6-cup (1.5-L) baking dish. In a food processor, blend remaining ingredients until smooth. Pour over cranberries and bake for 30 – 40 minutes, until top of gratin is an even golden brown colour.

Serve gratin warm, dusted with icing sugar.

NOTES

✧ "Gratin" refers to anything topped with breadcrumbs and butter or cheese and then browned, so this definitely qualifies!

✧ Cranberries are loaded with natural pectin (which is why cranberry sauce sets so firmly). Add them to your next fruit pie or cobbler to help set the juices of your other fruits. Do bear in mind that fresh cranberries have more pectin than frozen.

✧ Fresh cranberries can keep in the refrigerator for up to 2 months, and if you're not going to use them in that time simply toss the bag in the freezer as is.

Cranberry Clafouti

Individualizing this dessert effortlessly dresses it up, especially with a little ice cream on top!

Prepare the Cranberry Gratin (see page 51), but pour mixture evenly among 8 ramekins. Bake for 25–30 minutes, glaze with a little melted apricot jelly and serve dusted with icing sugar and a large scoop of vanilla ice cream.

Cranberry Mille Feuilles

PASTRY CREAM

1 cup	250 mL	milk
1 tsp	5 mL	vanilla extract
4	4	egg yolks
2 Tbsp	25 mL	sugar
7½ tsp	37 mL	cornstarch
		dash salt
4½ tsp	22 mL	unsalted butter
1 Tbsp	15 mL	brandy (optional)
2 Tbsp	25 mL	whipping cream

CRANBERRIES

2 cups	500 mL	cranberries, fresh or frozen
6 Tbsp	90 mL	water
¾ cup	175 mL	sugar
1	1	vanilla bean
½ tsp	2 mL	cinnamon
2 Tbsp	25 mL	brandy or rum

PUFF PASTRY

1	1	pkg frozen puff pastry, thawed
		icing sugar, for dusting

NOTES

◇ Weighting the puff pastry seems to defy its name and purpose, but doing so will create pastry layers that are level and flat, but still very flaky.

◇ Anything layered in this fashion can also be called a Napoleon.

◇ Slice this dessert with a serrated knife to cut through the flaky layers without shattering them.

"Mille feuilles" means "a thousand sheets," and this dessert's many flaky layers are filled with a creamy custard and fragrant cranberry filling. Irresistible!

FOR PASTRY CREAM, bring milk and vanilla extract to a simmer over medium heat. In a bowl, whisk together egg yolks, sugar, cornstarch and salt. Whisking egg mixture constantly, gradually add milk, a ladle at a time to the egg mixture until all the milk has been added. Pour mixture back into pot and return to medium heat. Whisking vigorously, bring mixture up to a simmer. Due to the cornstarch, pastry cream will thicken quickly, about 3–4 minutes. Remove from heat and, still whisking, stir in butter (this will help halt the cooking process). Stir in brandy, cover surface of pastry cream with plastic wrap and chill completely. Whip cream to medium peak and fold in. Chill until ready to assemble.

FOR CRANBERRIES, simmer cranberries with water, sugar, scraped seeds and pod of vanilla bean and cinnamon, stirring occasionally, until most cranberries have "popped," 15–20 minutes. Remove from heat, stir in brandy and remove vanilla bean. Cover cranberries with plastic wrap placed directly on surface and chill until ready to assemble.

FOR PUFF PASTRY, preheat oven to 375°F (190°C). Cut puff pastry into 3 equal pieces and keep 2 chilled while rolling first. On a lightly floured surface, roll out puff pastry into a square about 8 inches (20 cm). Trim edges with a ruler to create straight lines (or use bottom of a cake pan). Place on a parchment-lined baking sheet. Repeat with remaining 2 pieces (you should be able to fit 2 squares on 1 baking sheet). Chill for 10 minutes. Dock pastry with a fork and place a sheet of parchment over rolled dough. Place another baking sheet on top of pastry for weight and press down gently. Bake for 12 minutes. After 12 minutes, remove top baking tray and parchment and bake for 10–12 minutes more, until puff pastry is an even golden brown colour. Allow to cool.

To assemble, place one pastry square on a platter. Fill a piping bag with a large plain or star tip and fill with pastry cream. Pipe cream over pastry square, covering completely, but without going right to the edges (the weight of remaining layers will fill out cream). Lay second puff square over pastry cream. Gently spread cranberry filling over square. Top with last layer of pastry. Dust top of mille feuilles with icing sugar.

Currants

Dried currants are quite different from the fresh red or black variety that makes such lovely jams. Dried currants are actually a daintily proportioned grape that has been dried. They plump up beautifully, but because of their small size do not overwhelm the dessert.

Currant Rice Pudding

SERVES 6

3 cups	750 mL	milk
2 cups	500 mL	water
4	4	strips lemon zest
4$^{1}/_{2}$ tsp	22 mL	vanilla extract
$^{3}/_{4}$ cup	175 mL	short grain rice
$^{1}/_{3}$ cup	75 mL	dried currants
3 Tbsp	45 mL	sliced almonds, lightly toasted
$^{2}/_{3}$ cup	150 mL	sugar
1	1	egg yolk (optional)
		cinnamon, for garnish

I like the contrast of texture in this dessert. The creamy custard produced by the starch in the rice is accentuated by the quick crunch of toasted almonds. The currants serve to round the whole dish out.

Heat milk and water with lemon zest and vanilla to just below a simmer and stir in rice. Simmer, uncovered, for 10 minutes, stirring occasionally. Remove lemon peel. Add the currants, almonds and sugar and simmer 5 – 10 minutes more, testing rice for doneness. Remove from heat and stir in egg yolk. Spoon into a serving dish and sprinkle with cinnamon. Serve warm or chilled.

NOTES

❖ Short grain rice such as arborio or Japanese sushi rice is best for this recipe because it easily absorbs liquid and releases starches.

❖ The egg yolk adds a custard consistency and taste in this recipe, but can be omitted.

❖ Rice has always been my nemesis — even a professional chef has a food that eludes them. I tend to either overcook or undercook my rice, but I find that this recipe produces a perfect result every time!

[Switch Up]

Brûlée Rice Pudding

My friend Holly's mum used to make her rice pudding this way, and once I tasted it I immediately found the appeal. To melt sugar on any dessert doubles the comfort level!

Prepare Currant Rice Pudding (see page 54). Preheat oven to 400°F (200°C). Combine $^1/_4$ cup (50 mL) brown sugar with $^1/_2$ tsp (2 mL) cinnamon and sprinkle over rice pudding. Bake for 10 – 12 minutes until brown sugar melts on top of pudding. Serve immediately.

Caramel Butter Tarts

CRUST

2¹/₄ cups	550 mL	pastry flour
¹/₂ tsp	2 mL	salt
³/₄ cup	175 mL	lard or vegetable shortening
1 tsp	5 mL	lemon juice
1	1	egg
4–6 Tbsp	50–90 mL	cold water

FILLING

1 cup	250 mL	dried currants
¹/₂ cup	125 mL	hot water
¹/₄ cup	50 mL	unsalted butter, room temperature
¹/₂ cup	125 mL	dark brown sugar, packed
2	2	eggs
1 tsp	1 mL	vanilla extract
¹/₂ tsp	2 mL	white vinegar
		dash cinnamon
¹/₄ cup	50 mL	corn syrup
¹/₂ cup	125 mL	maple syrup

An über-Canadian treat, butter tarts are one of my husband's favourites, further patriated by the use of maple syrup instead of straight corn syrup.

FOR CRUST, preheat oven to 375°F (190°C). Combine flour and salt and cut in lard until coarse and crumbly. Whisk lemon juice and egg and mix into dough until it just comes together. Wrap and keep at room temperature while preparing filling.

FOR FILLING, soak currants in hot water for 10 minutes and drain. Set aside. Cream together butter and sugar and stir in eggs. Mix in vanilla, vinegar and cinnamon. Whisk in corn syrup and maple syrup.

On a lightly floured surface, roll out pastry to just shy of ¹/₄ inch (5 mm) thick. Cut 6-inch (15-cm) rounds from pastry and line ungreased muffin tins, pressing in well. Sprinkle a few currants in each shell and pour in filling, to half-fill shells. Bake tarts for 18 – 22 minutes, until filling is set. Allow to cool before removing from tin.

CARAMEL SAUCE

MAKES ABOUT 1 CUP (250 ML)

1 cup	250 mL	sugar
1 Tbsp	15 mL	golden corn syrup
1 tsp	5 mL	lemon juice
1/4 cup	50 mL	water
3/4 cup	175 mL	whipping cream
1 Tbsp	15 mL	unsalted butter
2 tsp	10 mL	vanilla extract

FOR CARAMEL SAUCE, bring sugar, corn syrup, lemon juice and water to a boil over high heat in a covered heavy-bottomed saucepan. Do not stir! Remove lid once sugar is boiling and let sugar cook, brushing sides of the pot with cool water once or twice (let wet brush almost touch the boiling sugar), until it's an amber colour. Remove from heat and slowly whisk in cream (watch out for rising steam). Stir in butter and vanilla. Let cool for 20 minutes before serving. Caramel sauce can be prepared ahead and chilled until ready to serve. Simply heat in microwave to warm.

To serve, place butter tart on plate and drizzle with caramel sauce. Butter tarts will keep up to a week in an airtight container (if they last that long).

NOTES

✧ I normally don't bake with lard, but this is one of my exceptions. To truly replicate the tarts your Grandma made, lard is a necessity. If you plan on eating the whole batch in one sitting (as, I am embarrassed to say, I have done), I recommend using vegetable shortening.

✧ It's best to whisk the filling by hand just until mixed. I find using electric beaters overmixes and creates too much air, which can cause the filling to separate as it bakes.

✧ Of course, the currants can be replaced by pecans, chocolate chips or nothing at all.

Dates

The first time I tasted a Medjool date was at a dinner hosted by the family of an Italian friend. They were served only with a large hunk of Parmesan cheese and a knife. That contrast between the salty cheese and the succulent sweet date was to die for!

Date Squares

MAKES 1 8-INCH (20-CM) SQUARE PAN
16 SQUARES

These are super-stacked squares. Loads of filling and crunchy layers make for a satisfying treat with a cup of tea or glass of milk.

FILLING

3 cups	750 mL	pitted dates
4¹/₂ tsp	22 mL	orange zest
4¹/₂ tsp	22 mL	unsalted butter
1 cup	250 mL	water

CRUMBLE

2¹/₂ cups	625 mL	rolled oats (regular or quick cook)
1¹/₄ cups	300 mL	all purpose flour
1 cup	250 mL	golden brown sugar, packed
2 tsp	10 mL	cinnamon
¹/₂ tsp	2 mL	salt
1 cup	250 mL	unsalted butter, melted

FOR FILLING, place all ingredients in a pot and bring up to a boil. Remove from heat and let dates soak until they're at room temperature. Purée until smooth and set aside.

FOR CRUMBLE, preheat oven to 350°F (180°C). Grease an 8-inch (20-cm) square pan and line bottom with parchment paper so that the paper hangs over the edge of the pan on 2 sides. Combine oats, flour, brown sugar, cinnamon and salt. Stir in butter and blend until it's an even crumbly texture. Press half the crumble into the bottom of prepared pan. Spread date filling over base and top with remaining crumble (not pressing). Bake for 40 – 45 minutes, until the top begins to brown. Allow to cool before cutting into squares.

NOTES

❖ Be sure to buy pitted dates. I bought unpitted dates once and what a racket they made in the food processor!

❖ Overhanging parchment paper in your cake and loaf pans allows you to lift out your squares or loaves easily.

❖ Tempting as it may be to cut the squares while they're warm, let them cool completely for smoother slicing.

Date Squares with Cranberry Coulis

CRANBERRY COULIS

MAKES ABOUT 2 CUPS (500 mL)

2 cups	500 mL	fresh or frozen cranberries
²/₃ cup	150 mL	sugar
¹/₂ cup	125 mL	water
2 tsp	10 mL	brandy
1 tsp	5 mL	vanilla extract

Add a flash of colour to your Date Squares with a tart Cranberry Coulis. Serve the square with a scoop of ice cream and ta-da!

Combine all ingredients in a saucepan and bring up to a simmer. Cook over medium-low heat, stirring occasionally, until the cranberries are tender (most will burst). Purée and strain, adding additional water if necessary. Chill before serving.

Date Crostata

FILLING

2 cups	500 mL	pitted dates, roughly chopped
1¹/₂ cups	375 mL	apple cider
³/₄ cup	175 mL	red wine
¹/₄ cup	50 mL	golden brown sugar, packed
2	2	cinnamon sticks
		dash ground cloves

CRUST

³/₄ cup	175 mL	unsalted butter at room temperature
¹/₂ cup	125 mL	sugar
1	1	egg
1 Tbsp	15 mL	sour cream
2¹/₄ cups	550 mL	all purpose flour
1 tsp	5 mL	anise seed, whole or ground
¹/₂ tsp	2 mL	salt

CREAM CHEESE

4 ounces	125 g	cream cheese at room temperature
2 Tbsp	25 mL	sugar
¹/₂ tsp	2 mL	vanilla extract

1 egg mixed with 2 Tbsp (25 mL) water for glazing

I like this tart because it transports so well. The cookie-like crust is very stable with its dense fruit filling. I also like that a lattice-top is created without actually weaving the pastry.

FOR FILLING, combine all ingredients in a saucepan and bring up to a boil over medium-high heat. Reduce heat to medium-low and simmer, stirring often, until dates have absorbed liquid and thickened, about 15 minutes. Cool to room temperature and remove cinnamon sticks.

FOR CRUST, cream together butter and sugar until smooth. Stir in egg and sour cream. In a separate bowl, combine flour, anise seed and salt and add to butter mixture. Mix just until dough comes together. Shape into 2 discs, wrap and chill for 20 minutes.

FOR CREAM CHEESE, beat cream cheese until smooth, then stir in sugar and vanilla and set aside.

Preheat oven to 350°F (180°C). On a lightly floured surface, roll out first disc to just under ¹/₄ inch (5 mm) thick and line a 9-inch (23-cm) removable-bottom tart pan (round or square), trimming edges. Spread cream cheese evenly on bottom of tart shell. Dollop date filling over cream cheese layer and spread evenly. Roll remaining pastry disc to just less than ¹/₄ inch (5 mm) thick and cut 12 strips, each ³/₄ inch (2 cm) wide. Lay six pastry strips over date filling, spacing evenly across tart. Lay remaining six strips crosswise over first layer of strips and trim excess dough from edges. Brush pastry with egg wash and bake tart on a baking tray for 40 – 50 minutes, until a rich golden brown. Cool tart for at least an hour before serving.

Tart can be served chilled or at room temperature.

NOTES

◊ The apple cider and red wine are certainly unique additions, and make for a smooth filling that's not overly sweet. When you add the liquid it will look like a lot, but those dates will absorb it all as it slowly simmers.

◊ Anise seed has a gentle licorice flavour. Use crushed fennel seed if anise is unavailable, or omit if you choose.

◊ Try serving this dessert with a glass of Madeira wine, which has a dried fruit taste that matches nicely with the dates.

Pineapples

It used to be a big treat in my house growing up when Dad would sit at the kitchen table and pare a pineapple, taking care to remove every trace of eyes. Now golden pineapple is widely available and Dad has one less kitchen chore because you can buy pineapples ready-peeled.

Pineapple Carrot Cake

This is one of those staple recipes that everyone needs in their repertoire.

FOR CAKE, preheat oven to 325°F (160°C). Grease an 8-inch (20-cm) square pan. Whisk together oil, brown sugar, eggs, maple syrup and grated ginger. In a separate bowl, sift flour, baking powder, baking soda, salt and cinnamon and blend into wet mixture. Stir in carrot and pineapple and pour into prepared pan. Bake $1^{1}/4 - 1^{1}/2$ hours until a tester inserted in the centre of the cake comes out clean. Allow to cool completely before icing.

FOR ICING, beat cream cheese with butter. Beat in icing sugar until smooth and stir in vanilla. Spread over top of cake and chill until ready to slice.

CAKE

$^3/4$ cup	175 mL	vegetable oil
$^3/4$ cup	175 mL	golden brown sugar, packed
3	3	eggs
$^1/4$ cup	50 mL	pure maple syrup
2 tsp	10 mL	grated fresh ginger
$1^2/3$ cups	400 mL	all purpose flour
1 tsp	5 mL	baking powder
$^1/2$ tsp	2 mL	baking soda
$^1/2$ tsp	2 mL	salt
1 tsp	5 mL	cinnamon
2 cups	500 mL	grated carrot
1 cup	250 mL	pineapple, diced or crushed, fresh or tinned (drained)

ICING

4 ounces	125 g	cream cheese at room temperature
$^1/4$ cup	50 mL	unsalted butter at room temperature
$1^1/2$ cups	375 mL	icing sugar, sifted
$1^1/2$ tsp	7 mL	vanilla extract

NOTES

◇ Pineapple is a symbol of hospitality, taken from the southern United States, where sea captains would show they had returned from their voyage by pegging a pineapple to their gate post. This signaled that guests were welcome to come and visit.

◇ I favour a nut-free carrot cake, but $^2/3$ cup (150 mL) of chopped walnuts would make a delicious addition.

◇ Try baking these as muffins for a morning treat.

◇ Check the ripeness of a pineapple by tugging a leaf at the crown. If it comes away freely, then the fruit is ripe.

Pineapple Carrot Mini Cakes

MAKES 6 MINI CAKES

ICING

4 ounces	125 g	cream cheese at room temperature
1/4 cup	50 mL	unsalted butter at room temperature
6 ounces	175 g	white chocolate, melted
1 1/2 cups	375 mL	icing sugar, sifted
1 1/2 tsp	7 mL	vanilla extract

Making individual cakes with icing enriched with a little white chocolate makes for fancy presentation of a favourite dessert. I've even prepared this recipe for a wedding cake, as it has great crowd appeal.

FOR CAKE, prepare cake recipe and bake in 6 greased ring molds that are 2³/₄ inches (7 cm) in diameter (wrap foil around molds to hold batter and place a disc of parchment in the bottom). Bake for 40 minutes.

FOR ICING, beat cream cheese and butter together. Beat in melted white chocolate and icing sugar until smooth and stir in vanilla.

To assemble, remove cakes from ring molds. Cut cakes in half horizontally. Frost top of bottom cake layer with ¹/₄-inch-thick (5-mm) icing. Lay remaining cake half on top. Spread icing on top of cake. Repeat with remaining 5 cakes. Keep chilled until ready to serve.

Tropical Nougat Glacée

PRALINE

¹/₂ cup	125 mL	sugar
2 Tbsp	25 mL	water
¹/₂ cup	125 mL	hazelnuts, lightly toasted and peeled

NOUGAT GLACÉE

5	5	egg yolks
²/₃ cup	150mL	sugar
6 Tbsp	90 mL	water
1¹/₄ cups	300 mL	whipping cream
2	2	egg whites
¹/₃ cup	75 mL	sugar
1 Tbsp	15 mL	pineapple juice
¹/₂ cup	125 mL	candied pineapple, diced
¹/₄ cup	50 mL	candied papaya, diced
¹/₄ cup	50 mL	candied mango, diced
¹/₄ cup	50 mL	sweetened coconut

This is the French version of the Italian "semifreddo." It's ultra-rich and quite sweet, a cross between a mousse and an ice cream. This is a favourite among a few of my friends and I like to make it when they're over for dinner.

FOR PRALINE, bring sugar and water to a boil. Boil until liquid is a light golden colour, brushing down the sides of the pot with water. Remove from heat and stir in hazelnuts. Spoon onto a parchment-lined and greased cookie sheet and let cool. Crack into pieces and pulse in food processor until fine, but still crumbly. Set aside.

FOR NOUGAT, whip egg yolks in a mixer fitted with the whisk attachment or with electric beaters until thick and foamy, about 5 minutes. Bring ²/₃ cup (150 mL) sugar and water to a boil over high heat. Cook sugar to 270°F (140°C), hard ball stage, 7 – 9 minutes. It should not colour. Pouring the hot sugar down the side of the bowl, whisk sugar into whipped egg yolks. Increase speed to high and whip until mixture is thick, pale and doubled in volume, 3 – 4 minutes. Let cool.

Whip cream to soft peaks and chill. Whip egg whites until foamy and gradually add ¹/₃ cup (75 mL) sugar and whip to stiff peaks. Pour pineapple juice over diced candied fruits and let it soak in. Fold whipped cream into egg yolk mixture, then fold in egg whites. Fold in praline, fruits and coconut and pour into 11 x 7-inch (2-L) pan (you can line with plastic wrap, but it's not essential). Freeze overnight.

To serve, immerse pan in hot water for 10 seconds then place serving plate on top and invert to unmold. Slice or spoon glacée into dishes.

NOTES
❖ If you can't find candied mango or papaya, dried fruit works just fine.

❖ The caramelized sugar praline adds a delicious crunch to this dessert if it's served the day you make it. After a day, the caramel melts and becomes a syrupy swirl. Both are equally delicious.

❖ My cheater version of this dessert is to sprinkle brown sugar on fresh pineapple slices, broil and then serve with a scoop of ice cream on top.

Bananas

I like serving banana desserts in the dead of winter, when I want to remind myself that somewhere the sun is shining on sandy beaches (and also because so many other fruits are bland and woody at that time of year).

Phyllo Wrapped Bananas

SERVES 4

1/4 cup	50 mL	dried cherries
4 ounces	125 g	cream cheese at room temperature
2 Tbsp	25 mL	sugar
1/2 tsp	2 mL	vanilla extract
8	8	sheets phyllo pastry
1/3 cup	75 mL	unsalted butter, melted
2 ounces	50 g	semisweet chocolate, roughly chopped
4	4	small bananas
3 Tbsp	45 mL	rum (optional)

CHOCOLATE SAUCE

MAKES ABOUT 1 CUP (250 ML)

1 cup	250 mL	water
2/3 cup	150 mL	sugar
1/2 cup	125 mL	Dutch process cocoa powder
1 tsp	5 mL	instant coffee
1/2 cup	125 mL	whipping cream

This dessert sounds too good to be true. It is easy to make, and I get such rave reviews every time I make it — from kids and grown-ups!

Preheat oven to 350°F (180°C). Soak dried cherries in hot water for 5 minutes to soften, then drain. Beat cream cheese until smooth and stir in sugar and vanilla extract.

Working with one sheet of phyllo pastry at a time (keep remaining phyllo completely covered under a damp towel), cut sheet in half. Brush first half with butter, place second half on top and brush with more butter. Repeat process with another sheet of phyllo cut in half. Spread 2 Tbsp (25 mL) cream cheese in the centre of the pastry. Place 4 1/2 tsp (22 mL) chopped chocolate and a sprinkle of dried cherries over cream cheese. Peel banana, cut in half and place pieces next to each other on top of filling and sprinkle with rum. Fold end edges of pastry in over banana. Roll up banana to create a square package and place on an ungreased baking sheet. Repeat with remaining bananas. Baste parcels with butter and bake for 15–20 minutes, until golden brown.

FOR CHOCOLATE SAUCE, bring water and sugar to a boil for 3–5 minutes. Sift cocoa powder and whisk in with instant coffee and return to a boil. Reduce heat to medium-low, add cream and whisk until sauce thickens, about 3 minutes. Chill until ready to serve and reheat in microwave before serving.

Slice diagonally across and serve with a scoop of ice cream. Drizzle with chocolate sauce and enjoy!

Banana Phyllo Tart

MAKES 1 8-INCH (20-CM) TART
SERVES 6

Feel like showing off a little? This tart looks incredible presented at the table, but still uses all the previous recipe's tasty ingredients.

Prepare dried cherries and cream cheese filling as on page 64.

Preheat oven to 400°F (200°C). Brush the sides of an 8-inch (20-cm) springform pan with melted butter. Line the bottom and sides of the pan with 5 sheets of the phyllo, buttering each piece as you layer. Allow phyllo to drape over the sides. Keep aside 3 layers for the top. Place filling inside the pan and fold in overhanging phyllo. Butter the remaining phyllo sheets, scrunch them and place on top of filling. Brush with butter. Bake for 20 minutes, until phyllo is golden.

To serve, pool a bit of warm chocolate sauce onto plate, slice wedge of banana phyllo tart and arrange over sauce.

NOTES

◇ When bananas ripen, they emit ethylene gas. If you have pears or avocados that are too firm, place them beside a bunch of bananas and they'll ripen faster.

◇ If you don't have cream cheese for the filling in this recipe, try using peanut butter for a childhood flashback.

◇ Having guests over? Make these roll-ups ahead of time, seal them in a plastic bag or container and then bake when you're ready to indulge.

Banana Rum Crème Brûlée

CHOCOLATE BOTTOM

¼ cup	50 mL	unsalted butter
4 ounces	125 g	semisweet chocolate, chopped
2 Tbsp	25 mL	coffee (optional)
2 Tbsp + 2 tsp	25 mL + 10 mL	golden corn syrup
½ cup	125 mL	sugar
½ cup	125 mL	cocoa powder, sifted
¼ tsp	1 mL	salt
⅓ cup	150 mL	whipping cream
1 tsp	5 mL	vanilla extract

CRÈME BRÛLÉE

4 cups	1 L	whipping cream
2	2	vanilla beans
12	12	egg yolks
1 cup	250 mL	sugar
¼ cup	50 mL	rum

BANANAS

2	2	bananas
3 Tbsp	45 mL	rum
½ cup	125 mL	sugar

Now this is something different. Instead of baking this crème brûlée in individual ramekins, I prepare it in a large baking dish. When I crack into the caramelized sugar and banana layer and smoothly scoop through the custard, I surprise everyone with a secret chocolate layer hidden beneath.

FOR CHOCOLATE BOTTOM, melt butter and chocolate together in a bowl placed over a pot of gently simmering water, stirring regularly. Stir in coffee, if using, and corn syrup. Add sugar, cocoa powder and salt and blend. Add cream and vanilla and continue stirring until sugar is dissolved. Pour chocolate sauce into bottom of 11 × 7-inch (2-L) baking dish.

FOR CRÈME BRÛLÉE, heat cream with the scraped seeds and pods of vanilla beans to just below a simmer. In a bowl, whisk together egg yolks, sugar and rum. Place bowl over a pot of simmering water and whisk vigorously until eggs are doubled in volume and hold a ribbon when the whisk is lifted. Remove from heat. Slowly pour cream into egg mixture, whisking constantly until all the cream has been added. Return cream to pot and stir with a wooden spoon over medium-low heat until cream has thickened and coats the back of a spoon, about 5 minutes. Remove from heat and strain. Pour brûlée filling over chocolate sauce in baking pan. Bake in a pan filled halfway up outside of brûlée dish with boiling water for 50 – 60 minutes. Remove dish from water bath, cool to room temperature, then chill for at least 3 hours before serving.

FOR BANANAS, slice lengthwise and place on top of custard mixture. Sprinkle with rum. Sprinkle with sugar and torch with a blowtorch or broil for one minute, with the oven door open a crack. Serve immediately.

NOTES

◇ I like this particular chocolate sauce recipe for this dessert because it stays smooth upon baking and remains somewhat fluid after chilling.

◇ A water bath or "bain marie" as it's often called is important for cooking custard, to ensure an even and insulated setting of the eggs for a silky-smooth result.

◇ If you moisten the sugar on top of the brûlée with a little mist of water it will melt and caramelize more evenly.

citrus

LEMONS | MORE LEMONS | LIMES | ORANGES | GRAPEFRUITS

Lemons

Lemon desserts are one of the finest ways to finish a meal. Their tartness cleanses the palate and the light flavour is not overwhelming, especially after a large meal. I always included at least one lemon dessert on my menu at the restaurant.

Lemon Thumbprint Cookies

MAKES ABOUT 2 DOZEN COOKIES

1 cup	250 mL	unsalted butter at room temperature
1/2 cup	125 mL	sugar
2	2	egg yolks
2 Tbsp	25 mL	lemon zest
1 Tbsp	15 mL	lemon juice
1/4 tsp	1 mL	salt
1 Tbsp	15 mL	cornmeal
2 1/2 cups	625 mL	all purpose flour
1/4 cup	50 mL	pistachios or walnuts, finely chopped
1/3 cup	75 mL	lemon marmalade

My Grandma used to make these dainty cookies for me, and fill them with raspberry jam. The cornmeal brings out the delicate lemon colour, to make these even more eye-catching.

Preheat oven to 350°F (180°C). Cream together butter and sugar until smooth. Add egg yolks, zest and juice. Combine salt, cornmeal and flour in a separate bowl, add to butter mixture and blend. Shape teaspoonfuls of cookie dough into balls and dip bottoms into chopped nuts. Place on a parchment-lined or greased baking sheet, leaving one inch between cookies and press an indentation in centre of cookie. Bake for 15 – 18 minutes, until nuts brown slightly.

While cookies are still warm, fill centres with little dollops of marmalade and allow to cool.

NOTES

◇ For chewier filled cookies, spoon in marmalade before baking.

◇ The coating of nuts protects the cookie from browning, while toasting up nicely itself.

◇ Of course, any jam would work nicely in these cookies. Why not use a few jams for a colour variety on your cookie plate?

Lemon Thumbprint Cookies with Sparkling Lemonade Floats

SPARKLING LEMONADE FLOATS

1/2 cup	125 mL	fresh lemon juice
1/2 cup	125 mL	sugar
2 cups	500 mL	cold water
2 cups	500 mL	sparkling wine, prosecco or club soda
		vanilla ice cream
1/2 cup	125 mL	fresh blueberries, and/or raspberries
		lemon slices and mint sprigs, for garnish

I used to love floats when I was a little kid, and these are a great adult version.

Stir together lemon juice and sugar with cold water.

To assemble, place scoops of ice cream into 6 tall glasses and pour lemonade over to fill the glass $3/4$ of the way. Top each glass with sparkling wine and garnish with berries, lemon slices and mint. Serve with cookies on the side (see page 71).

Caramel Dipped Orange Almond Biscotti 157–158

Warm Lemon Sponge

LEMON CURD

1/3 cup	75 mL	fresh lemon juice
3	3	eggs
1	1	egg yolk
1/2 cup	125 mL	sugar
1/2 cup	125 mL	unsalted butter, cut into pieces
1 tsp	5 mL	lemon zest

LEMON SPONGE

3	3	eggs
1/2 cup	125 mL	sugar
1/2 cup	125 mL	all purpose flour
1/4 tsp	1 mL	baking powder
1/4 tsp	1 mL	salt
1/4 cup	50 mL	unsalted butter, melted
1/2 tsp	2 mL	vanilla extract
1 tsp	5 mL	lemon zest
2 tsp	10 mL	lemon juice

A warm lemon dessert is such a delightful surprise, and a delicious contrast to typically cool citrus desserts. I favour this treat in mid-winter, after a cozy meal of roast or stew.

FOR LEMON CURD, whisk together lemon juice, eggs and yolk, and sugar. Whisk in butter and add lemon zest. Place bowl over a pot of simmering water and whisk steadily, but gently, until curd becomes thick and pale and creamy, about 10–15 minutes. Remove from heat and chill until ready to use.

FOR LEMON SPONGE, preheat oven to 350°F (180°C). Grease and sugar 6 5-ounce (150-mL) ramekins, and place a disc of parchment paper at the bottom of each ramekin. Warm eggs in their shells (see notes). Whip eggs and sugar in a mixer fitted with the whisk attachment until very pale and airy, about 10–15 minutes. Sift together dry ingredients. Combine butter, vanilla, zest and juice and set aside. Reduce speed on mixer to medium and add dry ingredients quickly, but not all at once, until almost blended. Add butter mixture, and mix just until blended.

Spoon cake mixture evenly among ramekins, leaving 1/2 inch (1 cm) at the top for expansion. Spoon a generous dollop of lemon curd into the centre of each cake. There is no need to press it in as it will sink a little during baking. Bake for 20–25 minutes until cake is golden brown and springs back when you touch it.

To serve, turn warm cake out onto a plate (you can serve it right side up or upside down). Dust top with icing sugar and serve with a piped bit of remaining chilled lemon curd beside it. Blueberries and blackberries make a great garnish.

NOTES

◇ Warm eggs whip to fuller volume than cold eggs. I place my eggs in their shells in a bowl, cover with hot tap water and let them sit for a few minutes. Then they're ready to use.

◇ Always use fresh lemon juice in your desserts — you can taste the difference from bottled. When I can, I buy lots of lemons, juice them at once and freeze the juice in plastic containers for later use.

◇ For ease in entertaining, you can prepare this dessert ahead of time fully, chill and then warm in the microwave.

More Lemons

The proof is in the pudding — lemon desserts are so popular that I needed to add more recipes!

Lemon Squares

MAKES 1 8-INCH (20-CM) SQUARE PAN
16 SQUARES

The only challenge I find in making this sweet treat is that you have to be patient and let the squares chill completely before slicing.

FOR CRUST, preheat oven to 350°F (180°C) and butter and line the bottom of an 8-inch (20-cm) square baking pan with parchment paper. Combine flour, salt, cornmeal and icing sugar. Cut in butter until dough is the texture of coarse meal (it will be crumbly). Press dough into pan and bake for 15–18 minutes, until it just begins to colour around the edges. Allow to cool.

FOR FILLING, whisk together all filling ingredients until smooth and pour over crust.

Bake for 25–30 minutes, until set with a visible crust on top of the squares.

Allow to cool at room temperature for 20 minutes, then chill for at least 2 hours, preferably longer, before slicing.

CRUST

1 cup	250 mL	all purpose flour
1/4 tsp	1 mL	salt
1/4 cup	50 mL	cornmeal
1/4 cup	50 mL	icing sugar
1/2 cup	125 mL	unsalted butter

FILLING

4	4	whole eggs
2	2	egg yolks
1 1/3 cups	325 mL	sugar
1/4 cup	50 mL	whipping cream or buttermilk
1/2 cup	125 mL	lemon juice
2 tsp	10 mL	lemon zest
1 tsp	5 mL	baking powder

NOTES

◇ The baking powder is the secret to great lemon squares. It reacts with the lemon juices, fizzes away as it bakes and creates that sweet crunchy crust atop the squares.

◇ Remember that any trimmings or crumbs that may fall are calorie free, but only to the cook that made them!

Lemon Squares with Berries and Lemon Sabayon SERVES 6

FRUIT

1 cup	250 mL	fresh strawberries, washed, hulled, quartered
1/2 cup	125 mL	fresh raspberries
1/2 cup	125 mL	fresh blueberries
1/2 cup	125 mL	fresh blackberries
1/4 cup	50 mL	limoncella liqueur
2 tsp	10 mL	lemon zest

SABAYON

4	4	egg yolks
1/4 cup	50 mL	sugar
1/4 cup	50 mL	white wine
1/4 cup	50 mL	lemon juice
2 Tbsp	25 mL	whipping cream, optional

Sabayon is a light-as-air sauce that, when made with lemon juice instead of the traditional Marsala wine, is a delightful dessert on its own over fresh berries!

FOR FRUIT, toss berries with limoncella and zest and set aside. Make no further than 2 hours in advance.

FOR SABAYON, prepare a pan with 2 inches (5 cm) of simmering water on the stove. In a metal bowl, whisk together egg yolks, sugar, wine and lemon juice. Place the bowl over the pan of water, holding the bowl with a dry towel, and whisk vigorously until the mixture triples in volume and leaves a ribbon when the whisk is lifted. Remove from heat. If you're preparing the sabayon in advance and you wish to chill it, whisk in the whipping cream and chill until ready to serve (up to a day ahead).

To serve, cut lemon squares and dust with icing sugar. Serve with berries and spoon sabayon over fruit and squares.

Lemon Mousse Cake

SPONGE

6	6	eggs
1 cup	250 mL	sugar
1 cup	250 mL	all purpose flour
1/4 tsp	1 mL	baking powder
1/4 tsp	1 mL	salt
1/2 cup	125 mL	unsalted butter, melted
1/2 tsp	2 mL	vanilla
2 Tbsp	25 mL	lemon juice
2 tsp	10 mL	lemon zest

SYRUP

3 Tbsp	45 mL	sugar
1 Tbsp	15 mL	lemon juice
2 Tbsp	25 mL	water

MOUSSE

4 1/2 tsp	22 mL	powdered gelatin
1/2 cup	125 mL	lemon juice
1 Tbsp	15 mL	lemon zest
1 cup	250 mL	whipping cream
3	3	eggs
1/3 cup	75 mL	sugar

NOTES

❖ This cake recipe is a traditional genoise sponge, often used in classic tortes and wedding cakes. The cake itself freezes very well (just don't put your 12-pound turkey on top of it).

❖ I save the cake trimmings from this recipe and either freeze them in a bag for trifle "in a pinch," or grind them into crumbs to line my pie shells before I add fruit (prevents a soggy crust).

❖ The lemon mousse is spectacular on its own. I pour into wide-mouthed wine glasses and top with berries.

Yes, you *can* make a perfectly finished cake! By pouring a tart lemony mousse onto the outside of the cake, you create a flawless dessert!

FOR SPONGE, preheat oven to 350°F (180°C). Line the bottom of an 8-inch (20-cm) springform pan with parchment but do not grease pan. Warm eggs in their shells in a bowl of hot water for 2–3 minutes. In a mixer or with an electric beater, whip eggs with sugar over high speed for 15 minutes. Sift together flour, baking powder and salt. In a separate bowl mix butter, vanilla, lemon juice and zest. With the mixer on medium-low speed, add flour mixture all at once. Let mix 30 seconds and add butter mixture all at once. Pour batter into pan and bake for 30 – 40 minutes, until cake springs back when you touch it. Allow to cool in pan.

FOR SYRUP, heat sugar, lemon juice and water together until sugar dissolves. Set aside.

FOR MOUSSE, soften gelatin in lemon juice with lemon zest added. Whip cream to soft peaks and chill. Warm eggs in their shells in warm water for 2–3 minutes. Whip eggs with sugar on high speed for 5 minutes. While eggs are whipping, melt gelatin mixture over low heat, stirring. When eggs have doubled in volume, fold in whipped cream by hand. With mixer on low speed, add gelatin mixture and blend for 10 seconds.

To assemble, place an 8-inch (20-cm) ring mold (or springform pan ring) on a plate. Trim sponge cake to 6 inches (15 cm) in diameter and slice into 2 horizontally. Place one disc inside the mold. Brush lightly with lemon syrup. Pour half the mousse over the cake, letting it spill over the sides. Spread mousse with a palette knife, getting mousse into every space. Place second cake disc on top of mousse and brush with syrup. Pour the rest of the mousse on top and spread evenly. Chill for at least 3 hours, preferably overnight.

Removing the mold is easy with the use of a blow dryer! Blow hot air over metal ring to warm slightly. Gently lift mold (if it seems to be sticking, keep warming with the dryer.) You will have a cake with sharp edges and perfect sides! Garnish cake in the centre with fresh berries.

Limes

Margaritas, anyone? That richly floral scent of limes always transports me back to my vacation in Mexico…aaaahh. I even have lime-accented perfume that I wear in winter when I need a pick-me-up.

Lime Pots de Crème

MAKES 6 5-OUNCE (150-ML) SERVINGS

2¼ cups	550 mL	whipping cream
3	3	egg yolks
2	2	whole eggs
½ cup	125 mL	sugar
¼ cup	50 mL	lime juice
4½ tsp	22 mL	lime zest

This is a great finish to a spicy meal!

Preheat oven to 325°F (160°C). Heat cream over medium-low heat to just below a simmer. Whisk together egg yolks, whole eggs, sugar, lime juice and zest. Gradually pour the cream over the egg mixture, stirring constantly until all cream has been added. Skim any foam off the surface of the custard. Arrange 6 5-ounce (150-mL) custard cups in a baking pan with a 2-inch (5-cm) lip. Pour the custard into the cups, and skim off any bubbles that occur. Set the baking pan on the open oven door and carefully pour boiling water around the cups, filling about halfway up the cups. Bake for 40 – 45 minutes, until custard jiggles just slightly in the centre when moved. Remove cups from water bath and let cool to room temperature for 20 minutes, then chill at least 2 hours before serving.

NOTES

❖ If you're trying to decide between making a lemon dessert or a lime dessert, remember that limes rarely have seeds, so they make for easier juicing!

❖ You cannot substitute the whipping cream in this recipe with a lower fat cream. Acidic ingredients curdle anything below 30% milk fat.

❖ A few slices of ripe mango certainly would add a colourful garnish.

Lime Pots de Crème with Crushed Raspberries

CRUSHED RASPBERRIES

MAKES ABOUT 1 CUP (250 ML)

2 cups	250 mL	fresh raspberries
1/4 cup	50 mL	sugar
2 tsp	10 mL	lime juice
1 tsp	5 mL	lime zest

Crushed raspberries sounds so appealing, doesn't it? This adds that little extra sparkle to an already luscious dessert.

Place raspberries in a bowl with sugar, lime juice and zest. Let sit for 5 minutes, then stir with a fork to crush the berries slightly (but do not purée them).

To serve, spoon crushed raspberries over Lime Pots de Crème (see page 77) and serve immediately.

Key Lime Pie

CRUST

3 cups	750 mL	chocolate cookie crumbs
1 cup	250 mL	sweetened coconut
1/2 tsp	2 mL	salt
3/4 cup	175 mL	unsalted butter

FILLING

3	3	7-ounce (213-mL) tins condensed milk
12	12	pasteurized egg yolks (or fresh yolks)
1 1/2 cups	375 mL	fresh lime juice
4 1/2 tsp	22 mL	lime zest

CANDIED LIME SLICES

2	2	limes
1 cup	250 mL	sugar
1 cup	250 mL	water
		sugar for sprinkling

ZESTED BLUEBERRY SAUCE

MAKES 2 CUPS (250 ML)

2 cups	500 mL	blueberries, fresh or frozen
3/4 cup	175 mL	sugar
1 Tbsp	15 mL	lime zest
1 Tbsp	15 mL	lime juice

This key lime pie recipe follows the traditional technique of *not* baking the filling. The acidity in the lime juice "cooks" the eggs as the filling chills. Pasteurized egg yolks are best for this recipe, but fresh eggs also can be used.

FOR CRUST, preheat oven to 375°F (190°C). Combine chocolate cookie crumbs, coconut and salt. Stir in melted butter and blend to an even, crumbly texture. Press crust into an ungreased 9-inch (23-cm) springform pan. Bake for 7–8 minutes, until scent of chocolate is noticeable. Allow to cool.

FOR FILLING, whisk together all ingredients until smooth and pour into baked pie shell. Chill for at least 4 hours before slicing.

FOR CANDIED LIME SLICES, slice limes into thin rounds. Blanch in a pot of boiling water for 2 minutes, then drain. In a saucepan, combine sugar and 1 cup (250 mL) water, bring up to a simmer and add lime slices. Simmer for about 10–15 minutes, until white pith looks translucent. Drain and spread out on a cooling rack over a baking tray to dry for about an hour. Coat limes with sugar and store in an airtight container, layered between parchment or plastic until ready to use.

FOR BLUEBERRY SAUCE, bring to a simmer 1 1/2 cups (375 mL) of the blueberries, sugar, lime zest and juice. Simmer for 15 minutes and remove from heat. Purée sauce with a hand blender or in a food processor. Add remaining blueberries and return to a simmer. Sauce can be served warm or chilled.

To serve, garnish with candied lime slices and serve blueberry sauce on the side.

NOTES

❖ When purchasing limes, or any other citrus fruit for that matter, shop for ones that are heavier than they look. They'll be juicier.

❖ Key limes are actually more of a yellow tone than green. Whether you use actual key limes or traditional limes, expect only a pale yellow-green pie filling.

❖ This pie presents well in the springform pan, but can also be prepared in a large 10-inch (25-cm) pie plate.

Oranges

It may be the one colour I don't wear well, but the fruit sure does make for some spectacular desserts. Whether using perfumey tangerines or mandarins, or more intense and bitter Seville oranges, I use orange when I want a change from lemon. It's a good flavour to use in spring, when berries may not be ripened yet but you can't bear the sight of another apple!

Tangerine Meltaways

COOKIES

³/₄ cup	175 mL	unsalted butter, room temperature
1 cup	250 mL	icing sugar, sifted
2 Tbsp	25 mL	tangerine zest
3 Tbsp	45 mL	fresh tangerine juice
1 Tbsp	15 mL	vanilla
1³/₄ cups	425 mL	all purpose flour
2 Tbsp	25 mL	cornstarch
¹/₄ tsp	1 mL	salt

GLAZE

2 Tbsp	25 mL	tangerine juice
6 Tbsp	90 mL	icing sugar
1 Tbsp	15 mL	unsalted butter, melted

My Mom brought this recipe back from a trip to Charleston, South Carolina and we both make it often. Enjoy these with a tall glass of iced tea, as they would in the South.

FOR COOKIES, cream together butter and icing sugar until smooth. Stir in tangerine zest, juice and vanilla. In a separate bowl, sift together flour, cornstarch and salt. Stir into butter mixture, shape into logs, wrap and chill for 1 hour.

Preheat oven to 325°F (160°C). Slice ¹/₄-inch (5-mm) rounds and place on a parchment-lined baking sheet. Bake for 12 – 15 minutes and allow to cool.

FOR GLAZE, whisk together juice, icing sugar and melted butter. Pour glaze over cookies to cover, or dip tops of cookies into glaze and set on a cooling rack to dry, about 1 hour.

NOTES

⬧ If tangerines are not in season, regular navel oranges work just fine.

⬧ The glaze for these cookies goes on shiny but dries with a matte finish.

⬧ When I make hot apple cider, I like to add a good splash of orange juice along with my cinnamon sticks — really adds zip.

Tangerine Meltaways with Minted Granita

MINTED TANGERINE GRANITA
MAKES 4 CUPS (1 L)

4 cups	1 L	fresh tangerine juice
1 cup	250 mL	sugar
3 Tbsp	45 mL	lemon juice
1 Tbsp	15 mL	mint

Granita is a great option for a cool treat that doesn't require an ice cream maker. This refreshing "ice" makes a delicious aperitif with a little Campari poured over it in a tall glass.

Heat tangerine juice with sugar and lemon juice just to dissolve. Remove from heat and stir in mint. Place in a container that offers some surface area, so the granita will freeze faster. Freeze for 6 hours. If you can, give the granita a stir twice, after the first and second hour in the freezer (but don't worry if you can't).

Scrape granita up with a fork, to create the granular texture, then scoop with a spoon. Serve with Tangerine Meltaways on the side (see page 80).

Orange Bavarian Torte

CAKE

1¼ cups	300 mL	pastry flour
1½ tsp	7 mL	baking powder
		dash salt
2	2	egg whites
½ cup	125 mL	milk
1 tsp	5 mL	vanilla
1 Tbsp	15 mL	orange zest
¼ cup +2 Tbsp	50 mL + 25 mL	unsalted butter at room temperature
⅔ cup	150 mL	sugar

ORANGES AND SYRUP

2	2	navel oranges
1 cup	250 mL	sugar
1 cup	250 mL	water

BAVARIAN CUSTARD

2 Tbsp +2 tsp	25 mL + 10 mL	powdered gelatin
3 Tbsp	45 mL	cold water
2 cups	250 mL	milk
2 cups	250 mL	half-and-half cream
1	1	vanilla bean
1 Tbsp	15 mL	orange zest
1¼ cups	300 mL	sugar
8	8	egg yolks
2 cups	500 mL	whipping cream
¼ cup	50 mL	orange liqueur
2 Tbsp	25 mL	candied orange slices, chopped

This is a great special occasion cake. Without having to fuss with icing or decorating, this cake presents spectacularly with its orange slices shining as they nestle within an orange-scented custard.

FOR CAKE, preheat oven to 350°F (180°C) and grease and flour an 8-inch (20-cm) cake pan. Sift together flour, baking powder and salt. Whisk together egg whites, milk, vanilla and zest. Cream together butter and sugar until fluffy. Add dry ingredients alternately with milk mixture, starting and finishing with flour. Scrape batter into pan and spread until it is level. Bake for 30 minutes, until a tester inserted into the centre of the cake comes out clean. Allow to cool 10 minutes in the pan, then turn out onto a rack and cool completely.

FOR ORANGES AND SYRUP, slice oranges thinly with a serrated knife and blanch for 1 minute in boiling water. Strain and cook in sugar mixed with 1 cup (250 mL) fresh water for about 20 minutes, until pith takes on a clear appearance. Drain, reserving some of the liquid for brushing the cake.

FOR BAVARIAN CUSTARD, stir gelatin with cold water to soften and set aside. Heat milk and half-and-half cream with scraped seeds from vanilla bean and orange zest. In a separate bowl, whisk together sugar and egg yolks. Slowly add hot cream mixture to eggs, whisking constantly. Return cream to pot and, stirring constantly over medium heat, cook custard until it coats the back of a spoon. Remove from heat and strain. Stir in gelatin to melt. Chill custard until just below room temperature, but not set, about 1 hour.

✧ A Bavarian custard is a classic pastry technique (they make you practice this one repeatedly at cooking school). The custard is thickened by eggs, set with gelatin and given body with whipped cream. You often see it made with unique fruit flavours and colours such as black currant and passion fruit.

✧ Keep this torte in its springform mold until you're ready to serve it. If you're making this dessert, then you're most likely entertaining and have a very full fridge. You can stack other plates on top of the pan and know your fabulous dessert won't get dented.

Whip cream to medium peaks and stir in liqueur and chopped candied orange. Fold cream into custard in 3 additions.

To assemble, line a 10-inch (25-cm) springform pan with plastic wrap. Lay orange slices around bottom of pan, curving up and around sides. Pour in custard to cover oranges. Level cake with a knife if necessary and gently set it on top of custard with bottom of cake facing up. Brush with orange syrup. Wrap and chill torte for at least 6 hours, preferably overnight.

To serve, turn springform pan onto a plate and remove. Peel off plastic and present.

Grapefruits

What a funny name for a fruit that is not at all related to grapes! It gets its name, of course, because the fruit grows in clusters that resemble bunches of grapes.

I always opt for pink grapefruit, for dessert and for breakfast — white grapefruit is more bitter, and I don't need to comment on the colour!

Grapefruit Watermelon Granita

SERVES 4

1 cup	250 mL	fresh pink grapefruit juice
1/3 cup	75 mL	sugar
1 cup	250 mL	watermelon pulp, seedless
1/4 cup	50 mL	citrus vodka
		fresh mint, for garnish

Refreshing and fat-free, this is a satisfying dessert after grilled fish and a giant salad. How healthy!

Bring grapefruit juice and sugar up to a simmer and stir until sugar is dissolved. Remove from heat and cool. Purée grapefruit syrup with watermelon and strain. Stir in vodka and freeze. After an hour, stir granita, and then stir twice more before it's frozen.

To serve, scrape up granita granules with a fork and spoon into dessert glasses. Garnish with fresh mint.

NOTES

◇ Only heat the grapefruit juice enough to just melt the sugar. If the juice gets too warm its colour will fade and it will lose its fresh taste.

◇ For a kid-friendly version, just omit the vodka.

◇ I find this treat often appeals to those who are not big dessert-eaters. It can also double as an intermezzo, to cleanse the palate between rich courses.

Grapefruit Granita with Lime Cream Serves 4

LIME CREAM

¹/₂ cup	125 mL	whipping cream
2 tsp	10 mL	sugar
2 tsp	10 mL	lime juice
¹/₂ tsp	2 mL	finely grated lime zest

A simple flavoured cream paired with the icy granita creates a "creamsicle" effect that is as irresistible as it was when we were kids.

FOR LIME CREAM, whip cream to soft peaks and fold in sugar, juice and zest. Chill until ready to serve.

To serve, scrape up granita granules with a fork and spoon into dessert glasses. Top granita with a small dollop of lime cream and garnish with fresh mint.

Grapefruit Pavlovas

MERINGUE

4	4	egg whites at room temperature
3/4 cup	175 mL	sugar
1 tsp	5 mL	cornstarch
1/2 tsp	2 mL	lemon juice or white vinegar

CREAM

1 cup	250 mL	whipping cream
3 Tbsp	45 mL	crème fraîche or sour cream
2 Tbsp	25 mL	sugar
5 Tbsp	70 mL	raspberry juice, from fresh or frozen berries

GRAPEFRUITS

3	3	pink grapefruits

TOPPING

1/2 cup	125 mL	sugar
1 Tbsp	15 mL	corn syrup
2 Tbsp	25 mL	water

NOTES

◊ Whipping egg whites on one setting below high will produce a meringue of fuller volume with a stronger structure that will hold its shape better because finer air bubbles are produced.

◊ It's the combination of cornstarch and lemon juice that gives the pavlova its crunchy outside and marshmallow-like centre.

◊ My inspiration for this dessert is my favourite way to eat grapefruit in the morning — cut in half, sprinkled with brown sugar and broiled!

The delight of these pavlovas not only resides in their lovely pink colour, but also in their caramelized crunch topping, which slowly dissolves as it comes in contact with the sweet pink grapefruit juices. Call it "Pavlova Brûlée" for lack of a better term! Meringues are sensitive to humidity so keep in mind that a meringue that takes 25 minutes to bake on a dry winter's day could take 40 minutes or longer on a warm summer's day.

FOR MERINGUE, preheat oven to 225°F (105°C). Trace 8 4-inch (10-cm) circles onto 2 sheets of parchment paper (4 per sheet). Turn paper over (so ink doesn't transfer to meringues) and line baking sheets. In a mixer fitted with the whisk attachment or with electric beaters, whip egg whites until frothy. While whipping, gradually add in sugar and beat to form stiff peaks. By hand, gently fold in cornstarch and lemon juice or vinegar until incorporated. Spread onto traced circles. Bake for 25 – 40 minutes — if meringue starts to show signs of colouring, reduce oven temperature slightly. Allow to cool.

FOR CREAM, whip cream to medium peaks and fold in crème fraîche or sour cream, sugar and raspberry juice. Chill until ready to serve.

FOR GRAPEFRUITS, cut away skins and pith with a serrated knife. Slice into thin discs (you should get about 16 slices).

FOR TOPPING, in a small saucepan, bring sugar, corn syrup and water up to a boil. Cook without stirring for 3 – 4 minutes, until it turns light brown. Pour syrup onto a sheet of greased parchment paper and allow to cool. Pulse the caramelized sugar in a food processor to grind finely.

To serve, place each meringue onto a serving plate and dollop with raspberry cream. Arrange 2 grapefruit slices over cream and sprinkle generously with sugar. Serve immediately.

sugar

HONEY | BROWN SUGAR | BUTTERSCOTCH

Honey

Honey is the one flavour we can't seem to synthetically replicate (have you ever seen "artificial honey?").

Honey Roasted Fruit

SERVES 6

3 | 3		ripe Bartlett or Bosc pears, peeled, halved and cored
2 | 2		apples, peeled, cored, and sliced in 1-inch (2.5-cm) rounds
3 | 3		plums, halved and pitted
3 | 3		apricots, halved and pitted
³/₄ cup | 175 mL		cranberries, blackberries or pitted sweet cherries
1 cup | 250 mL		honey
1 cup | 250 mL		white wine
2 | 2		cinnamon sticks or 1¹/₂ tsp (7 mL) ground cinnamon
2 tsp | 10 mL		fresh grated ginger

Serve in a large baking dish or roast in individual cups. Either way, the flavours meld together beautifully as it cooks (and the house will smell fantastic).

Preheat oven to 375°F (190°C). Toss all the fruit in a large bowl. Heat honey with wine, cinnamon and ginger, to allow flavours to infuse. Pour honey mixture over fruit and toss to coat.

Arrange fruit in individual cups by first placing apple slices on the bottom and then arranging a pear half on top of each apple slice. Arrange remaining fruit around pears. Pour leftover honey syrup over fruit. Bake for 30 – 40 minutes, until fruit (pears particularly) is tender. Test by inserting a skewer into fruit. Serve warm.

NOTES

◇ Different honeys have distinct flavours. Buckwheat honey is deep and farmy, while clover honey is light and fruity.

◇ Try adding dried apricots or prunes to the fruit mix for wintry variation.

Honey Roasted Fruit with Honey Apple Sabayon

HONEY APPLE SABAYON

4	4	egg yolks
2 Tbsp	25 mL	honey
2 Tbsp	25 mL	sugar
¼ cup	50 mL	apple cider
¼ cup	50 mL	lemon juice
2 Tbsp	25 mL	whipping cream, optional

This sauce is like a lighter version of crème brûlée, with the emphasis on the fruit flavours.

Prepare a pan with 2 inches (5 cm) of simmering water on the stove. In a metal bowl, whisk together egg yolks, honey, sugar, cider and lemon juice. Place the bowl over the pot of water, holding the bowl with a dry towel, and whisk vigorously until the mixture triples in volume and leaves a ribbon when whisk is lifted. Remove from heat. If you're preparing sabayon in advance and you wish to chill it, whisk in whipping cream and chill until ready to serve.

To serve, spoon sabayon over warm Honey Roasted Fruit (page 91) and serve immediately.

Panforte with Crème Fraîche

³/₄ cup	175 mL	whole hazelnuts, peeled, toasted and chopped
³/₄ cup	175 mL	whole almonds, toasted and chopped
³/₄ cup	175 mL	candied orange peel, chopped
6 Tbsp	90 mL	candied lemon peel, chopped
6 Tbsp	90 mL	raisins
6 ounces	175 g	dark chocolate, bitter-sweet or semisweet, cut into pieces
6 Tbsp	90 mL	all purpose flour
1 tsp	5 mL	cinnamon
¹/₄ tsp	1 mL	allspice
¹/₄ tsp	1 mL	cloves
¹/₄ tsp	1 mL	nutmeg
		dash black pepper
²/₃ cup	150 mL	sugar
²/₃ cup	150 mL	honey
4¹/₂ tsp	22 mL	butter

CRÈME FRAÎCHE
MAKES 2 CUPS (500 ML)

2 cups	500 mL	whipping cream
2 Tbsp	25 mL	buttermilk or lemon juice

NOTES

✧ The easiest way to peel hazelnuts is to toast them at 350°F (180°C) on a cookie sheet for 12 minutes, cool, and then rub them in a colander. The skins will fall into the holes and you'll be left with the peeled nuts!

✧ Black pepper is a surprising spice to see in a dessert recipe, but its bite offsets the sweetness of the other flavours. It's also a great addition to poaching liquid for pears.

✧ The cooked sugar and honey cool quickly once all the chocolate, fruit and nuts are stirred in. Make sure you have your pan prepared and ready to go before you start.

✧ This is the Italian version of fruitcake. My parents visited Tuscany last year and brought some delicious samples for me to try. The results didn't last long!

Panforte in Italian means "strong bread" and is best eaten in smaller portions because of its sweet, rich flavour. The combination of dried fruits, nuts and chocolate cooked together with honey makes for a sweet ending, perfect after a holiday meal. Cut it into squares to eat as petits fours.

Preheat oven to 300°F (150°C). Butter and line bottom and sides of a 10-inch (25-cm) springform pan with parchment paper. Butter parchment (or spray with food release). In a large bowl, combine nuts, peel, raisins, chocolate, flour, and spices.

In pot over medium heat, cook sugar, honey and butter until it reaches a temperature of 245°F (118°C), 8–10 minutes. Working quickly, pour syrup over nut mixture, stirring until chocolate is melted. The panforte stiffens quickly, so immediately spoon mixture into pan and spread to edges. Bake for 30 minutes. Allow to cool in the pan completely. Wrap and store at room temperature.

FOR CRÈME FRAÎCHE, stir together cream and buttermilk or lemon juice. Place in a clear cup or bowl, preferably plastic. Cover with plastic wrap. Place bowl in hot water, up to the level of the cream and store in a warm place (near oven, radiator) for 24–48 hours. You will know when it's ready because you will see the thin-textured whey settled at the bottom. Chill before using, being sure to not stir whey into crème fraîche (it will thin out crème fraîche). To ensure whey does not become mixed in, gently scrape cream away from whey when spooning out.

To serve, cut panforte into slender wedges, 2 per plate, and serve with a spoonful of unsweetened crème fraîche.

Panforte can be kept in an airtight container for up to a month (honey is one of nature's best preservatives).

Brown Sugar

Brown sugar is made by adding back some of the molasses removed during the sugar refining process. The depth of colour of brown sugar indicates its strength of flavour — the lighter the colour, the milder the flavour, the darker the colour, the more intense. Just remember when measuring brown sugar to pack it into the measuring cup.

Brown Sugar Pound Cake

MAKES 1 9-INCH (3-L) BUNDT CAKE
SERVES 12 TO 16

CAKE

I cup	250 mL	unsalted butter, room temperature
2 cups	500 mL	golden brown sugar, packed
I cup	250 mL	granulated sugar
2 tsp	10 mL	vanilla extract
6	6	eggs, room temperature
3 cups	750 mL	pastry flour
1/2 tsp	2 mL	salt
I cup	250 mL	sour cream
1/4 tsp	1 mL	baking soda

GLAZE

6 Tbsp	90 mL	icing sugar
2 Tbsp	25 mL	browned and strained butter
I Tbsp	15 mL	water
I tsp	5 mL	vanilla

This is one of those staple recipes that I pull out when I need to feed a crowd. Sometimes I freeze half the cake when I only have to feed half a crowd.

FOR CAKE, preheat oven to 275°F (140°C). Grease and flour a 9-inch (3-L) bundt pan. In a mixer fitted with the paddle attachment, or with electric beaters, cream butter, sugars and vanilla on high speed until light and fluffy, scraping down sides often. Add eggs one at a time, beating after each addition. Sift together flour and salt. In a separate bowl combine sour cream and baking soda. Add flour and sour cream alternately to sugar mixture, beginning and ending with flour. Scrape cake batter into prepared pan. Bake for 20 minutes at 275°F (140°C), then turn up oven to 325°F (160°C) and bake for an additional 40–50 minutes or until a tester inserted in the centre of the cake comes out clean.

FOR GLAZE, stir icing sugar with browned and strained butter, water and vanilla.

Ice cake after it has cooled by drizzling glaze overtop.

NOTES
✧ "Bundt" means "gathering" in German and this is definitely a cake to feed a crowd.

✧ When flouring a pan after greasing, be certain to shake out excess flour.

✧ Dark brown sugar works as well as golden in this recipe, just the colour will vary. This is not the norm in most recipes — most recipes will specify which type of brown sugar to use.

Caramelized Pineapple Brown Sugar Cake

For a spectacular plated dessert, prepare the Brown Sugar Pound Cake (see page 94). Cut 8 4-inch (10-cm) discs of cake and place on a foil-lined baking sheet. Place a ring of fresh pineapple on each cake and sprinkle generously with brown sugar. Broil for 1 – 2 minutes, until sugar is melted. Serve immediately.

Sticky Bun Pudding

STICKY BUN DOUGH

2 tsp	10 mL	dry active yeast
1/4 cup	50 mL	warm water
1/2 cup	125 mL	milk at room temperature
1	1	egg at room temperature
2 Tbsp	25 mL	sugar
2 1/2 cups	625 mL	all purpose flour
1/2 tsp	2 mL	salt
1/2 cup	125 mL	unsalted butter at room temperature
4 ounces	125 g	cream cheese at room temperature

STICKY BUN FILLING

1 cup	250 mL	unsalted butter at room temperature
1 cup	250 mL	dark brown sugar, packed
1 Tbsp	15 mL	cinnamon
1/2 tsp	2 mL	nutmeg
1 cup	250 mL	pecans

BREAD PUDDING

4 cups	1 L	milk
1 Tbsp	15 mL	vanilla extract
1/4 cup	50 mL	sugar, + 2 Tbsp (25 mL) for sprinkling
1/4 cup	50 mL	dark brown sugar, packed
8	8	eggs

NOTES

✧ Store your brown sugar with a slice of bread in the tin to keep it moist.

✧ If using instant yeast in place of dry active yeast, you can skip the first step where yeast dissolves in liquid.

✧ I make this recipe and prepare the filling with a few ripe bananas mashed in — this makes a super-moist sticky bun.

This is a two-for-one recipe. The recipe for sticky buns is a great one on its own, but once transformed into a bread pudding — unbelievable!

FOR STICKY BUN DOUGH, dissolve yeast in water and allow to sit for 5 minutes. Add milk, egg and sugar and blend. Add flour and salt and mix for 1 minute to combine. Add butter and cream cheese and knead for 5 minutes on medium speed. Place dough in a lightly oiled bowl, cover and let rest 1 hour.

FOR STICKY BUN FILLING, combine butter, sugar, cinnamon and nutmeg. Chop pecans and add to mixture. Spread half the filling in a 13 x 9-inch (3.5-L) baking pan.

Preheat oven to 350°F (180°C). On a lightly floured surface, roll out dough into a rectangle 1/2 inch (1 cm) thick. Spread remaining filling over the dough and roll up lengthwise. Slice dough into 12 equal portions and arrange them in baking pan, leaving some room between buns. Allow to rise for 1/2 hour. Bake 30 minutes.

FOR BREAD PUDDING, let sticky buns dry overnight (or if you're in a hurry, chill in the fridge).

Preheat oven to 350°F (180°C). Remove buns from pan and slice across, creating spiral-looking slices. Butter a 13 x 9-inch (3.5-L) baking pan and arrange slices in pan. Heat milk and vanilla just to a simmer. In a bowl whisk together sugars and eggs. Adding a little at a time, whisk milk into eggs until it is all incorporated. Pour over buns and press down to let mixture soak in. Sprinkle top of pudding with sugar. Bake for 35–45 minutes, until centre of pudding springs back when pressed.

To serve, cut pudding into squares, or spoon from dish. Serve warm.

Butterscotch

Caramel is a constant favourite and I find butterscotch has had a resurgence in popularity over the past few years. Butterscotch is a softer, creamier version of caramel that coats the mouth as it slowly melts.

Butterscotch Bars

MAKES 1 8-INCH (20-CM) SQUARE PAN
16 SQUARES

BASE

¹/₄ cup	50 mL	unsalted butter, room temperature
¹/₂ cup	125 mL	granulated sugar
¹/₂ cup	125 mL	dark brown sugar, packed
2	2	eggs
¹/₂ tsp	2 mL	vanilla
1¹/₄ cups	300 mL	all purpose flour
¹/₂ tsp	2 mL	baking soda
¹/₂ tsp	2 mL	salt

BUTTERSCOTCH

¹/₂ cup	125 mL	unsalted butter
¹/₂ cup	125 mL	sugar
1 cup	250 mL	dark brown sugar, packed
¹/₂ cup	125 mL	golden corn syrup
¹/₄ cup	50 mL	water
¹/₂ tsp	2 mL	salt
1 cup	250 mL	walnut pieces
³/₄ cup	175 mL	unsweetened coconut
¹/₂ cup	125 mL	whipping cream
2 tsp	10 mL	vanilla extract
³/₄ cup	175 mL	chocolate chips

I wish I could tell you what a complete plate of these squares looks like, but I have yet to see such a thing. There's usually a line-up in the kitchen to get a bite right out of the tin.

FOR BASE, preheat oven to 350°F (180°C) and grease and line bottom of an 8-inch (20-cm) square pan with parchment paper. In a bowl, cream butter and sugars together. Add eggs and vanilla and beat until fluffy. In a separate bowl, combine flour, baking soda and salt. Add to butter mixture and stir until evenly blended. Spread batter into a prepared pan and bake for 20 – 25 minutes, to an even golden brown. Set aside to cool.

FOR BUTTERSCOTCH, in a saucepan, melt butter over medium heat. Stir in sugars, corn syrup, water and salt and increase heat to medium-high. When mixture reaches a boil, stir in walnut pieces and coconut. Simmer for 7 minutes, stirring often (mixture will become thick and darker in colour). Remove from heat and stir in cream and vanilla (watch for steam). Pour butterscotch over base and sprinkle with chocolate chips. Bake for 13 – 16 minutes, until bubbling around the edges. Allow to cool before cutting into squares or bars. Do not refrigerate.

Butterscotch Bars will keep up to 3 weeks in an airtight container.

NOTES

◊ In the United Kingdom, anything called "butterscotch" must contain 4% butter.

◊ Drizzle the top of the squares with melted chocolate for added flair.

◊ Do not chill these squares. Sugar liquefies in the fridge, and your squares would not look very square after a few hours.

Butterscotch Bars with Chai Coffee

CHAI COFFEE
SERVES 6

I cup	250 mL	whipping cream
2 Tbsp	25 mL	sugar
6 cups	1.5 L	dark roast brewed coffee
4	4	cardamom pods
4	4	whole star anise
3	3	whole cloves
2	2	cinnamon sticks
³⁄4 cup	175 mL	coffee liqueur or brandy
		ground cinnamon, for garnish

While Chai tea has become a current favourite, using the same spices in coffee is absolutely delicious, and adds a complexity that pairs well with the Butterscotch Bars.

Whip cream to soft peaks, fold in sugar and chill. Pour hot coffee into a saucepan. Crush cardamom pods and star anise and add to pot. Add cloves and cinnamon, and steep over low heat for 5 minutes. Strain. Fill each of 6 glasses with an ounce of coffee liqueur and top up with coffee. Top with whipped cream and a sprinkle of cinnamon. Serve with Butterscotch Bars (page 97) on the side.

Butterscotch Cream Pie

CRUST

2 cups	500 mL	all purpose flour
2 Tbsp	25 mL	ground pecans, toasted
1/4 tsp	1 mL	salt
1/2 cup	125 mL	unsalted butter, cut into pieces and chilled
2 Tbsp	25 mL	golden brown sugar, packed
1	1	egg yolk
4–6 Tbsp	50–90 mL	cold water

FILLING

1 cup	250 mL	pecan halves, lightly toasted
1 cup	250 mL	golden brown sugar, packed
1/3 cup	75 mL	all purpose flour
1 cup	250 mL	milk
3 Tbsp	45 mL	unsalted butter
1 Tbsp	15 mL	vanilla extract
1	1	egg yolk

TOPPING

1 cup	250 mL	whipping cream
2 Tbsp	25 mL	sugar
1 tsp	5 mL	vanilla extract
		chopped toasted pecans, for garnish

NOTES

✧ The addition of ground pecans and a little brown sugar to this basic pie dough adds taste and makes it easier to work with.

✧ Blind baking is the technique of weighting a pie crust that might have the tendency to bubble up, leaving no room for the filling. I use rice or dried beans and keep them in a coffee tin for re-use.

✧ Definitely use golden brown sugar in this recipe, for a milder, truly buttery taste. I made it once with dark brown sugar (it was all I had in the pantry at the time) and it was too dark and too strong tasting.

My husband, Michael, loves this recipe. His mum, Mae, would make butterscotch pie as a special treat. I've taken the liberty of adding pecans for a little spark.

FOR CRUST, combine flour, ground pecans and salt. Cut in butter to an even, crumbly texture. In a separate bowl, whisk brown sugar with egg yolk and 4 Tbsp (50 mL) water and add to flour. Mix just until dough comes together, adding a little more water if needed. Wrap and chill for 30 minutes. On a lightly floured surface, roll out dough to 1/8 inch (3 mm) thick. Line a 10-inch (25-cm) pie shell with dough and trim. Chill for 20 minutes.

Preheat oven to 375°F (190°C). Line pie shell with aluminum foil and weight with pie weights, rice or dried beans. Bake for 18–20 minutes, then remove foil and weights and bake for 5–7 minutes more, until centre of pie shell is dry and edges are lightly browned. Allow to cool.

FOR FILLING, line bottom of baked pie shell with toasted pecan halves. In a saucepan, mix brown sugar and flour together, crushing any large lumps of brown sugar. Whisk in milk until smooth. Stir filling over medium-low heat to start dissolving sugar, then stir in butter. Cook filling for about 8 minutes, stirring constantly, until it thickens. Remove from heat and scrape into a bowl. Stir in vanilla and egg yolk. Spread filling into pie shell. Chill for at least 2 hours before topping.

FOR TOPPING, whip cream to soft peaks and fold in sugar and vanilla. Spread evenly over butterscotch filling and garnish with chopped pecans. Chill until ready to serve.

Pie with filling can be made up to 2 days in advance, and topped up to 6 hours in advance.

chocolate

WHITE CHOCOLATE | MILK CHOCOLATE | COCOA
CLASSIC CHOCOLATE | MORE CHOCOLATE

White Chocolate

There's craving for chocolate and then there's craving for white chocolate, which is of the most extreme variety and requires prompt attention. I find I like to contrast the rich sweetness of white chocolate with a little something tart. It makes the dessert that much more palatable.

White Chocolate Brownies

1/3 cup	75 mL	unsalted butter, cut into pieces
6 ounces	175 g	white chocolate, chopped
2	2	eggs
1 cup	250 mL	sugar
2 tsp	10 mL	vanilla
1 cup	250 mL	all purpose flour
1/2 tsp	2 mL	baking powder
1/4 tsp	1 mL	salt
1/4 cup	50 mL	dried cranberries
1/2 cup	125 mL	walnut pieces (optional), lightly toasted
		icing sugar, for dusting

MAKES 1 9-INCH (23-CM) SQUARE PAN
12 TO 16 SQUARES

Otherwise known as Blondies, these brownies are dense, sweet and rich.

Preheat oven to 350°F (180°C). Butter and line a 9-inch (23-cm) square baking pan with parchment. Over a pot of just-simmering water, melt butter halfway. Add white chocolate and stir until melted. Allow to cool to room temperature.

In a mixer fitted with the whisk attachment or with electric beaters, whip eggs, sugar and vanilla until pale and thick. Reduce speed to medium and add chocolate mixture.

In a separate bowl, sift together flour, baking powder and salt and stir into egg mixture, by hand. Stir in dried cranberries and walnuts, if using, and spoon into prepared pan. Bake 45 minutes, until golden brown. Allow to cool completely before cutting and dust with icing sugar.

Brownies will keep for 4 – 6 days in an airtight container.

NOTES

✧ White chocolate is a bit of a misnomer, since it contains no chocolate liquor (the dark flavour component) but is instead made up of cocoa butter, milk and vanilla.

✧ White chocolate melts at about 6°F (2°C) lower than regular chocolate, so when melting, stir over barely simmering water or on medium heat in the microwave. Pull it off the heat before it has completely melted and let the heat of the bowl finish the job.

Mini White Chocolate Brownies with Chocolate Hazelnut Sour Cream

MAKES 24–30 BROWNIES

HAZELNUT SOUR CREAM

½ cup	125 mL	chocolate hazelnut spread
2 Tbsp	25 mL	sugar
¾ cup	175 mL	sour cream

Topped or served with a thick Hazelnut Sour Cream, these look just like dainty petits fours and make a great after-dinner nosh (or midnight snack).

Prepare the White Chocolate Brownie recipe (see page 103) and bake for 20–25 minutes in a greased mini muffin tin.

Cream chocolate hazelnut spread in a bowl and stir in sugar. Add sour cream and mix until blended. Pipe or spread onto brownies or dollop on the side.

Frozen White Chocolate Soufflé

RHUBARB

2 cups	500 mL	chopped rhubarb
1/2 cup	125 mL	sugar
2 tsp	10 mL	vanilla extract

MOUSSE

8 ounces	250 g	white chocolate, chopped
1 1/3 cups	325 mL	whipping cream
2	2	eggs, separated
2 Tbsp	25 mL	water
2 Tbsp	25 mL	brandy or rum
3 Tbsp	45 mL	sugar
		dash salt

This recipe looks like a spectacular baked soufflé without the effort or the worry of whether it will sink! Essentially a light, frozen mousse, the rhubarb flavour complements the white chocolate, making it quite a refreshing dessert.

FOR RHUBARB, simmer rhubarb, sugar and vanilla until soft. Purée and set aside to cool.

FOR MOUSSE, prepare 6 5-ounce (150-mL) ramekins by wrapping outsides with parchment rings that stand 2 inches (5 cm) above the lip of the ramekin. Secure parchment with butcher's twine or an elastic band.

Over a pot of simmering water (or in the microwave) melt chocolate, stirring constantly, and set aside to cool. Keep water simmering on the stove. Whip cream to soft peaks and chill. Whisk together egg yolks, water, brandy and 2 Tbsp (25 mL) sugar for 2 minutes, to warm eggs. Whisk chocolate into egg yolk mixture and let sit until it's at room temperature. Fold in whipped cream in 2 additions just until incorporated. Whip egg whites to medium peaks, and add 1 Tbsp (15 mL) sugar and dash of salt. Fold one-third into mousse followed by remaining two-thirds. Fold in rhubarb quickly.

Pour or spoon mousse into ramekins, filling up over the edge of the ramekin. Freeze overnight (or for at least 6 hours). To serve, simply remove parchment and garnish with a few fresh berries.

NOTES

❖ Without the rhubarb, this recipe works well as a regular chilled mousse. Pour into wine glasses or a nice serving dish and chill for 4 hours before serving.

❖ This follows a traditional mousse preparation of folding the whipped cream into the base and then the whipped whites last, as they are more volatile and need to be agitated least.

❖ In place of rhubarb, you could make this recipe just as delicious by using raspberry or apricot purée.

Milk Chocolate

I am guilty of picking out the milk chocolates in a box of mixed chocolates! The smooth consistency just goes down so easily! Because milk chocolate can sometimes be a challenge to locate, any of these recipes can be prepared using semisweet chocolate.

Chocolate Orange Pudding

SERVES 4

3 ounces	75 g	milk chocolate, chopped
2 cups	500 mL	milk
1 Tbsp	15 mL	orange zest
1/2 cup	125 mL	sugar
8	8	egg yolks
1/4 cup	50 mL	cornstarch
2 Tbsp	25 mL	cocoa powder
2 Tbsp	25 mL	unsalted butter
2 Tbsp	25 mL	orange liqueur, optional

Probably my favourite chocolate flavour combination, this is my personal comfort treat. Even when making hot chocolate, I like to put in a little orange peel or orange extract.

Melt chocolate over a pot of barely simmering water, stirring constantly (or melt in microwave, stirring every 20 seconds) and reserve.

Heat milk with orange zest over medium heat until it just comes to a simmer. Whisk together sugar, yolks, cornstarch and cocoa powder. Adding a little at a time, ladle milk into egg mixture, whisking constantly until all milk is added. Pour liquid back into pot and cook over medium heat, whisking constantly for about 3 minutes, until it thickens. Remove from heat immediately and scrape into bowl (to prevent pudding from continuing to cook). Stir in chocolate, butter and liqueur, if using, until fully incorporated.

If you wish to serve pudding in individual cups, pour into cups now and cover surface of each with plastic wrap (to prevent a skin from forming). Otherwise cover surface of pudding with plastic wrap and chill for an hour and a half until set.

Pudding can be made up to 2 days in advance. To serve, garnish with a dollop of whipped cream and a fresh orange slice.

NOTES

✧ Once the pudding starts to thicken, it does so rapidly. Be sure to have a bowl ready beside the stove to pour the pudding into and halt the cooking process.

✧ No need to limit the flavour combination to orange. Try almond, hazelnut or a little peanut butter.

Chocolate Orange Cream Pie

CHOCOLATE COOKIE CRUST

1½ cups	375 mL	chocolate cookie crumbs
2 Tbsp	25 mL	flour
2 tsp	10 mL	sugar
		dash salt
4 tsp	20 mL	unsalted butter, melted

ORANGE SPIKED CHANTILLY

1 cup	250 mL	whipping cream
4½ tsp	22 mL	sugar
2 Tbsp	25 mL	orange liqueur or zest of one orange
		chocolate shavings or cocoa powder (optional)

What a perfect way to dress up this pudding — to go from diner-style dessert to diner-style pie!

FOR CHOCOLATE COOKIE CRUST, preheat oven to 350°F (180°C). Combine cookie crumbs, flour, sugar and salt. Stir in butter and blend until crumbly. Spoon crust into an 8–inch (20-cm) springform pan or 2 4-inch (10-cm) pans and press firmly. Bake for 10 minutes and allow to cool. Prepare pudding filling as above and pour into shell while warm. Cover with plastic wrap and chill until set, about 2 hours.

FOR ORANGE SPIKED CHANTILLY, whip cream to soft peaks and stir in sugar and liqueur or orange zest.

Spread chantilly over pie filling and top with chocolate shavings or sift cocoa powder on top.

Milk Chocolate Almond Semifreddo

1 cup	250 mL	sliced almonds
1 Tbsp	15 mL	unsalted butter
		dash salt
7 ounces	225 g	milk chocolate, chopped
1 ⅓ cups	325 mL	whipping cream
2	2	eggs
¼ cup	50 mL	sugar
2 tsp	10 mL	vanilla extract
		dash almond extract
		cocoa powder, for dusting

Semifreddo means "half frozen" in Italian, and this dessert is a cross between a mousse and an ice cream. Need I say more?

Preheat oven to 350°F (180°C). On an ungreased baking sheet, toast almonds for 10 – 12 minutes, until light golden brown. Allow to cool.

Melt butter in a sauté pan over medium heat. Add almonds and salt and stir together until coated, about 4 minutes. Remove from heat. In a bowl over a pot of slowly simmering water (or in the microwave at high heat stirring every 20 seconds) melt chocolate, stirring constantly, and set aside. Keep pot of water simmering on the stove.

Whip cream to soft peaks and store in fridge until ready to use. Whisk together eggs, sugar, and extracts in a metal or glass bowl. Place bowl over simmering water and whisk constantly until doubled in volume, and whisk leaves a ribbon when lifted. Remove from heat. Whisk in melted chocolate and allow mixture to cool for about 10 minutes (so as to avoid melting whipped cream). Meanwhile, line a loaf pan with plastic wrap. Fold whipped cream into chocolate mixture in two additions until evenly incorporated. Fold in toasted almonds and pour mixture into loaf pan. Freeze overnight.

Semifreddo can be spooned or scooped, or unmolded and cut. To slice and serve, invert loaf pan onto a plate and remove pan and plastic wrap. Dust semifreddo with cocoa powder (turning on its sides to fully coat). Slice, wiping knife after every cut.

NOTES
◇ This dessert is delicious made with semisweet or with white chocolate.

◇ Toasting the almonds makes all the difference! And the little bit of salt that coats them offsets the sweetness of the chocolate for a perfect balance.

◇ Get creative and put the semifreddo mix into a nicely shaped mold for great presentation at the table.

Cocoa

There are two main types of cocoa powder. Dutch process cocoa has been alkalized, so some of the natural acidity present in cocoa has been removed, leaving a milder tasting cocoa that is darker in colour. Regular cocoa has a ruddy colour and is good in recipes that require leavening as its slight acidity reacts with the baking soda.

You probably won't have a recipe fail if you use one type of cocoa over another. If a recipe doesn't state which type to use, then whichever you have in your pantry should work just fine.

Cocoa Wafer Cookies

MAKES ABOUT 3 DOZEN

³/₄ cup	175 mL	unsalted butter at room temperature
1 cup	250 mL	icing sugar
6 Tbsp	90 mL	Dutch process cocoa powder
1 tsp	5 mL	vanilla extract
1	1	egg yolk
1 Tbsp	15 mL	milk
1¹/₂ cups	375 mL	all purpose flour
		dash salt
		dash baking powder
		icing sugar, for garnish

Sometimes simpler is better. These cookies are tender, tasty and not complicated to make. They are great for holiday cut-out cookies as well.

Beat butter until smooth and fluffy. Sift together icing sugar and cocoa powder over butter and beat in. Stir in vanilla, egg yolk and milk. Add flour, salt and baking powder to cocoa mixture and blend until incorporated. Shape dough into disc, wrap and chill for 20 minutes.

Preheat oven to 325°F (160°C). On a surface lightly dusted with icing sugar, roll out dough to ¹/₈ inch (3 mm) thick. Cut into desired shapes and transfer carefully to a parchment-lined baking sheet. Bake for 12 – 15 minutes, until cookies can be lifted easily away from the parchment. Allow to cool on baking sheet. Cookies can be dusted with icing sugar to finish.

Cookies will keep in an airtight container for 2 – 3 weeks.

NOTES

◇ Be certain to always sift your cocoa powder, even if making hot chocolate. It always has lumps!

◇ Rolling the cookies out in icing sugar instead of flour works well and ensures that your cookie dough won't take on added flour (which toughens cookies).

◇ I use these cookies as a garnish when I want to add a little "crunch" to a dessert, as in a custard or ice cream.

Chocolate Mint Cookies

MINT FILLING

1	1	egg white
1¾ cups	425 mL	icing sugar, sifted
2–3	2–3	drops peppermint extract

These are just too cool — they look store-bought but taste 100% homemade!

Prepare Cocoa Wafer Cookies (see page 109).

FOR MINT FILLING, put egg white in a bowl and beat in icing sugar, a few tablespoonfuls at a time, until a soft dough forms. Turn dough onto a surface dusted with icing sugar. Knead in remaining icing sugar and peppermint extract, until dough is no longer sticky.

To fill cookies, roll a teaspoon of dough into a ball and flatten a little. Sandwich between 2 cookies and press together to push icing to edges. Continue until all cookies have been filled.

Cookies can be glazed with chocolate to finish or dusted with icing sugar.

Cocoa Cupcakes with Chocolate Sorbet

CUPCAKES

1 1/3 cups	325 mL	dark brown sugar, packed
1/3 cup	75 mL	milk
6 Tbsp	90 mL	regular cocoa powder (not Dutch process), sifted
9 Tbsp	135 mL	unsalted butter, room temperature
1 tsp	5 mL	vanilla extract
2	2	eggs
2/3 cup	150 mL	all purpose flour
2/3 cup	150 mL	pastry flour
1 tsp	5 mL	baking soda
1/2 tsp	2 mL	salt
1/4 cup	50 mL	milk

GLAZE

3/4 cup	175 mL	whipping cream
6 ounces	175 g	semisweet chocolate, chopped
1/4 cup	50 mL	unsalted butter, room temperature

CHOCOLATE SORBET
MAKES ABOUT 4 CUPS (1 L)

1 cup	250 mL	milk
1 cup	250 mL	water
3/4 cup	175 mL	sugar
1/4 cup	50 mL	Dutch process cocoa powder, sifted
3 Tbsp	45 mL	corn syrup
1 Tbsp	15 mL	lemon zest
		dash salt
7 ounces	225 g	bittersweet chocolate, chopped

When testing this recipe, the leftovers never hung around long enough for me to wonder what to do with them! The chocolate sorbet is also quite nice on its own.

FOR CUPCAKES, preheat oven to 375°F (190°C) and line 24 muffin tins with paper cups. Stir together 2/3 cup (150 mL) brown sugar, 1/3 cup (75 mL) milk and cocoa powder over medium heat until well blended. Remove from heat. With a hand mixer, beat softened butter and remaining 2/3 cup (150 mL) of brown sugar into cocoa mixture until fluffy. Add vanilla and eggs and blend. In a separate bowl, sift together flours, baking soda and salt. Add alternately with remaining milk until all ingredients have been incorporated. Spoon into paper cups, filling halfway. Bake for 18 – 20 minutes, until a tester inserted in the centre of a cupcake comes out clean. Allow to cool.

FOR GLAZE, heat cream to just below a simmer and pour over chopped chocolate. Let sit for one minute then stir to smooth out. Stir in butter to melt in and thicken glaze. Pour over cupcakes while glaze is warm.

FOR CHOCOLATE SORBET, whisk together milk, water, sugar, cocoa, corn syrup, lemon zest and salt in a saucepan over medium heat until sugar is dissolved. Add chocolate and continue stirring until melted. Keep chocolate just below a simmer and stir until mixture is smooth, and visible chocolate grains dissolve away. Remove from heat and chill. Pour sorbet base into ice cream maker following manufacturer's instructions. Scrape sorbet into a container and freeze for at least 2 hours before serving.

Serve with cupcakes or in a dessert dish.

NOTES

◇ Cupcakes are a great variation on a traditional birthday cake — you can even stack them!

◇ To replace 1 ounce (25 g) of unsweetened chocolate, melt 3 Tbsp (45 mL) cocoa powder with 1 Tbsp (15 mL) unsalted butter.

◇ The glaze for these cupcakes is a ganache (what you find in the centre of truffles). If you find it is setting up before you finish glazing, just re-melt to liquid consistency in the microwave.

◇ If you don't have an ice cream maker, freeze sorbet until solid, then pulse in food processor or blender until smooth and return to freezer again until firm.

Classic Chocolate

When we say the word chocolate, there are certain fixed items that pop into our minds. For me, chocolate chip cookies is one and the other is a 1950's smiling image of June Cleaver holding a cake plate with a chocolate layer cake. She obviously didn't eat any of it herself, as she had a virtually invisible waistline!

Chocolate Chip Cookies

MAKES ABOUT 2 DOZEN

³/₄ cup	175 mL	unsalted butter, softened
I cup	250 mL	golden brown sugar, packed
¹/₄ cup	50 mL	granulated sugar
I	I	egg
2 tsp	10 mL	vanilla extract
2 cups	500 mL	all purpose flour
2 tsp	10 mL	cornstarch
I tsp	5 mL	baking soda
¹/₂ tsp	2 mL	salt
8 ounces	250 g	bittersweet chocolate, cut into chunks

Tried, tested and true. I have the empty glasses of milk to prove it.

Preheat oven to 350°F (180°C). Cream together butter and sugars until smooth. Add egg and vanilla and blend in. Stir in flour, cornstarch, baking soda and salt. Stir in chocolate chunks. Drop by tablespoons onto a greased baking sheet and bake for 8–10 minutes, until golden brown around the edges.

Let cool slightly and enjoy.

NOTES

◈ My secret ingredient for making chewy-centred cookies is cornstarch. If you want crispy cookies, omit the cornstarch and replace the baking soda with baking powder.

◈ If your butter is very soft, your cookies may spread flat. If just room temperature they will hold their shape better. If your butter is too soft, toss the prepared cookie dough in the fridge for 20 minutes or so just to firm it up a bit.

◈ The most challenging step in this recipe is "let cool slightly!"

Chocolate Chip Cookie Ice Cream Sandwiches

For an easy treat, scoop generous spoonfuls of softened vanilla ice cream between two chocolate chip cookies. Freeze until ready to serve. (The cookies have enough sugar in them that they will stay soft when frozen.)

Ultimate Chocolate Cake

MAKES 1 9-INCH (23-CM) CAKE
SERVES 10 TO 12

CAKE

¹/₂ cup	125 mL	unsalted butter, room temperature
1¹/₂ cups	375 mL	granulated sugar
¹/₂ cup	125 mL	golden brown sugar, packed
2	2	eggs
2 tsp	10 mL	vanilla extract
¹/₂ cup	125 mL	water
4 ounces	125 g	unsweetened chocolate, chopped
2 tsp	10 mL	espresso powder
1³/₄ cups	425 mL	pastry flour
¹/₄ cup	50 mL	cocoa powder
1 tsp	5 mL	baking soda
¹/₄ tsp	1 mL	salt
1 cup	250 mL	sour cream

ICING

2 cups	500 mL	unsalted butter, room temperature
1	1	egg yolk, optional
12 ounces	750 g	bittersweet or semisweet chocolate, chopped, melted and cooled to room temperature
2 tsp	10 mL	vanilla extract
¹/₄ tsp	1 mL	salt
2¹/₂ cups	625 mL	icing sugar, sifted

I can't even remember when I first started making this recipe, but it makes a great birthday cake.

FOR CAKE, preheat oven to 350°F (180°C). Butter and flour 2 9-inch (23-cm) round cake pans, shaking out excess flour. Cream butter and sugars together until fluffy. Beat in eggs and vanilla.

In a small pan stir water, chocolate and espresso powder over low heat until melted. Allow to cool slightly before beating into butter mixture.

Sift together flour, cocoa powder, baking soda, and salt and stir into batter alternately with sour cream. Divide evenly between the 2 pans and bake for 25 – 35 minutes, until a tester inserted in the centre of the cake comes out clean. Allow to cool 15 minutes in the pans, then turn cakes out onto a plate to cool completely.

FOR ICING, beat butter on high speed, scraping sides frequently, until light and fluffy. Reduce speed and beat in egg yolk, if using. Add melted chocolate and mix in. Add vanilla, salt and icing sugar and beat until smooth.

To ice the cake, top one layer with icing and spread. Place second cake layer on top. Ice the top of the cake and finish with the sides. Chill cake to set, but it is best stored at room temperature (you may omit egg yolk in icing, if desired).

NOTES

◇ Both sour cream and brown sugar are often found in chocolate cake recipes. They both add moisture while the sour cream tempers the sweetness of the cake.

◇ If your cakes have a rounded or peaked top to them (it often happens), trim a little off to level it. I freeze the scraps to turn into crumbs to coat the sides of cheesecakes.

◇ Adding the egg yolk to the icing creates a richer taste and a glossier finish. Don't worry, though, if you'd rather omit it. The recipe won't be compromised.

◇ Admittedly, this recipe calls for an extensive amount of butter, but remember, you are having just one slice of a very large cake! See, I can rationalize just about anything!

More Chocolate

There's no such thing as too much chocolate!

Nanaimo Bars

MAKES 1 8-INCH (20-CM) SQUARE PAN
9 TO 16 SQUARES

This recipe does appear to have a lot of ingredients, but Nanaimo Bars come together rather quickly. A friend of mine kept one in his pocket while skiing, for emergency fuel.

FOR BASE, preheat oven to 350°F (180°C). Grease bottom and sides of 8-inch (20-cm) square pan with vegetable oil or spray. Melt butter and stir in sugar. Sift cocoa powder into mixture and blend well. Whisk together egg and vanilla extract and add. Blend in chocolate cookie crumbs, coconut and chopped walnuts. Press into prepared pan and bake for 10 minutes. Allow to cool for 10 minutes then chill for 20 minutes.

FOR FILLING, beat butter by hand until smooth, then beat in custard powder. Stir in milk and vanilla, and add sifted icing sugar a cup at a time, combining well. Spread over base and chill while preparing topping.

FOR TOPPING, melt chocolate and butter over a pot of gently simmering water. Pour over vanilla filling and spread to cover evenly. Chill for 30 minutes.

To serve, slice with a hot, dry knife into 1-inch (2.5-cm) squares.

BASE

¹/₂ cup	125 mL	unsalted butter
¹/₄ cup	50 mL	sugar
5 Tbsp	70 mL	cocoa powder
1	1	egg
1 tsp	5 mL	vanilla extract
1¹/₂ cups	375 mL	chocolate cookie crumbs
1 cup	250 mL	unsweetened grated coconut
¹/₂ cup	125 mL	walnuts, toasted and chopped

FILLING

¹/₃ cup	75 mL	unsalted butter, room temperature
4¹/₂ tsp	22 mL	custard powder
¹/₄ cup	50 mL	milk
2 tsp	10 mL	vanilla
3 cups	750 mL	icing sugar, sifted

TOPPING

8 ounces	250 g	semisweet chocolate, chopped
2 Tbsp	25 mL	unsalted butter

NOTES

❖ Be sure to use oil to grease your pan instead of butter. Chilling the nanaimo bars would set the butter and make the squares impossible to remove from the pan.

❖ This recipe can be prepared without nuts. Just replace the nut portion with an equal amount of cookie crumbs.

❖ Custard powder can often be found in the grocery aisle with puddings and gelatin desserts if you can't find it in the baking aisle.

Cappuccino Nanaimo Bars

Dressing regular Nanaimo Bars up with a touch of coffee flavour makes them a great treat with a fresh pot of coffee. Just add 2 tsp (10 mL) of instant coffee powder to the filling mix and continue assembling as on page 115.

Triple Chocolate Mousse

BITTERSWEET CHOCOLATE MOUSSE

6 ounces	175 g	bittersweet chocolate, chopped
1/2 tsp	2 mL	gelatin powder
1/2 cup	125 mL	milk
1 1/4 cups	300 mL	whipping cream

WHITE CHOCOLATE MOUSSE

12 ounces	750 g	white chocolate, chopped
1/2 tsp	2 mL	gelatin powder
1/2 cup	125 mL	milk
1 cup	250 mL	whipping cream

MILK CHOCOLATE MOUSSE

10 ounces	300 g	milk chocolate, chopped
1/2 tsp	2 mL	gelatin powder
1/2 cup	125 mL	milk
1 cup	250 mL	whipping cream

DACQUOISE CRUNCH

2	2	egg whites
1/4 tsp	1 mL	cream of tartar
1/4 cup	50 mL	sugar
1/4 tsp	1 mL	vanilla extract
2 Tbsp	25 mL	ground hazelnuts
1/4 tsp	1 mL	cornstarch

NOTES

⬥ The weights of chocolate for each layer are different because each type of chocolate has a different degree of setting ability — white sets softest while dark sets firmest.

⬥ The Dacquoise Crunch is a nut meringue that adds depth and texture balance to the dessert. The dessert will still be very delicious if you're not in the mood to make the garnish.

⬥ As this recipe serves a large group (and uses a lot of chocolate), you can halve the recipe for a smaller group and build it in a loaf pan for attractive slices.

This dessert is silky and rich, and probably one of the easiest mousse techniques. All you need is a little time to let each layer set.

FOR BITTERSWEET CHOCOLATE MOUSSE, melt chocolate in a bowl resting over a pot of gently simmering water, stirring constantly, and remove from heat. Stir gelatin powder into milk and let sit for a minute. Heat milk (microwave is easiest) to just below a simmer and whisk into chocolate. Let cool to room temperature. Whip cream to soft peaks and fold into chocolate. Pour mousse into a plastic-wrap-lined 9-inch (23-cm) square pan at least 2 inches (5 cm) deep, spreading well into corners. Chill for at least 1 hour.

FOR WHITE CHOCOLATE MOUSSE, follow the same method as the bittersweet mousse: melt the chocolate, add gelatin to milk, heat the milk and stir in, let cool, whip cream and fold into chocolate. Spoon or pour gently over bittersweet mousse layer and chill for at least 1 hour.

FOR MILK CHOCOLATE MOUSSE, repeat the process, and pour mousse gently over white chocolate layer. Chill for at least 4 hours before serving.

FOR DACQUOISE CRUNCH GARNISH, preheat oven to 225°F (105°C) and line a baking tray with parchment paper. Whip egg whites with cream of tartar until foamy and add sugar gradually. Whip to stiff, glossy peaks. Stir in vanilla. Toss ground hazelnuts with cornstarch and fold into meringue. Spread gently on parchment paper. Bake for 40–50 minutes until dry but not browned. Allow to cool.

To serve mousse, invert pan onto a plate and peel off plastic. With a hot, dry knife slice squares of mousse and lift onto plates with a pie-lifter. Break Dacquoise Crunch into large pieces and place on mousse as garnish.

dairy

RICOTTA | YOGHURT | SOUR CREAM | WHIPPED CREAM | CREAM CHEESE

Ricotta

This may sound unsophisticated, but for me ricotta is a cottage cheese replacement. I dollop it on green salads, stir it into egg noodles with browned onions, and use it as a filling in breads and as a topping on pizza. For a dairy fanatic, ricotta is truly satisfying with its fresh, almost sweet taste.

Ricotta Peach Muffins

MAKES 12 MUFFINS

2¹/₂ cups	625 mL	all purpose flour
1¹/₂ tsp	7 mL	baking powder
¹/₂ tsp	2 mL	baking soda
¹/₂ tsp	2 mL	salt
1¹/₃ cups	325 mL	golden brown sugar, packed
¹/₂ cup	125 mL	creamy ricotta cheese
¹/₂ cup	125 mL	canola oil
2	2	eggs
1¹/₂ tsp	7 mL	vanilla extract
1 cup	250 mL	peaches, peeled and diced
2	2	peaches, sliced for garnish
		turbinado sugar, for sprinkling

This is a great use for the smooth, creamy ricotta that comes in a tub.

Preheat oven to 350°F (180°C). In a bowl, sift together flour, baking powder, baking soda and salt. In a separate bowl, blend together brown sugar, ricotta cheese, oil, eggs and vanilla. Add flour to brown sugar mixture and blend just until incorporated. Stir in diced peaches and spoon into a greased muffin tin. Arrange a few sliced peaches on each muffin and sprinkle tops generously with turbinado sugar. Bake for 35–40 minutes, until tops are golden brown and a tester inserted in the centre of a muffin comes out clean. Allow to cool for 10 minutes before removing from muffin pan.

NOTES

❖ Ricotta is one of the few ingredients where low-fat works as well in a recipe as regular. The choice is yours.

❖ Ricotta is traditionally the whey cheese remaining from the making of Provolone cheese.

❖ Raspberries or chopped rhubarb are great substitutions for peaches in this recipe.

Ricotta Peach Loaf with Cinnamon Ricotta Spread MAKES 1 9 × 5-INCH (2-L) LOAF

CINNAMON RICOTTA SPREAD
MAKES 1 CUP (250 ML)

1 cup	250 mL	creamy ricotta cheese
2 Tbsp	25 mL	sugar
1 tsp	5 mL	cinnamon
1 tsp	5 mL	grated orange zest

Imagine slathering a sweet cinnamon-scented spread over warm peach loaf. Mmmmmm! Now forget imagination and back to reality — you'd better get baking!

Prepare Ricotta Peach Muffin batter (see page 121) and scrape into a greased 9 x 5-inch (2-L) loaf pan. Bake for 45 – 55 minutes, until a tester inserted in the centre of the loaf comes out clean. Allow to cool for 15 minutes before removing from pan.

FOR CINNAMON RICOTTA SPREAD, combine all ingredients and chill until ready to use. To serve, spread a generous dollop onto warm slices of loaf.

Lemon Ricotta Pie

This is very much like an Italian-style cheescake. I like serving this after an Italian supper, when tomatoes and olives abound. When everyone thinks they can't have another bite, well they find they have room for just a little more!

FOR CRUST, combine flour, sugar, salt, lemon zest and cinnamon. Cut in the butter until the dough takes on an even crumbly texture, with some bits of butter still visible. Whisk together Marsala wine and egg yolk and add to flour mixture. Combine just until dough comes together. Shape into a disc, wrap and chill for an hour. On a lightly floured surface, roll out dough to 1/4 inch (5 mm) thick, and line an ungreased 9-inch (23-cm) springform pan so that pastry comes 2 inches (5 cm) up the sides. Chill dough while preparing filling.

FOR FILLING, mix Marsala, ricotta, cream, eggs, sugar, cinnamon, vanilla and almond extract in a bowl. Sift flour over top. Blend for 4 minutes, until very well combined. Place amaretti biscuits into a tea towel and crush. Sprinkle amaretti crumbs over chilled pastry shell. Spoon ricotta filling into pastry shell and spread evenly. Chill for 20 minutes.

Preheat oven to 350°F (180°C). Place pie on a baking tray and bake for 1 1/4 – 1 1/2 hours, until firm to the touch in the centre. Turn off the oven and open the oven door a crack. Leave pie in until oven is cool.

Chill completely before slicing.

CRUST

1 1/4 cups	300 mL	all purpose flour
1/4 cup	50 mL	sugar
1/2 tsp	2 mL	salt
2 tsp	10 mL	lemon zest
1 tsp	5 mL	cinnamon
1/2 cup	125 mL	unsalted butter, cut into pieces and chilled
2 Tbsp	25 mL	Marsala wine
1	1	egg yolk

FILLING

2 Tbsp	25 mL	Marsala wine
4 cups	1 L	dry ricotta cheese
3/4 cup	175 mL	whipping cream
4	4	eggs
9 Tbsp	135 mL	sugar
1 tsp	5 mL	cinnamon
1/2 tsp	2 mL	vanilla
1/4 tsp	1 mL	almond extract
5 Tbsp	70 mL	all purpose flour
1 cup	250 mL	amaretti biscuits

NOTES

❖ Dry ricotta usually comes wrapped in paper then packed in plastic. If unavailable, drain creamy ricotta (from a tub) through cheesecloth for at least 4 hours to achieve the correct consistency.

❖ The amaretti biscuits are a nice touch — they add flavour and serve to absorb liquid to keep the crust dry.

❖ I like serving this dessert with fruits soaked in wine, such as plums and cherries or berries.

Yoghurt

The popularity of yoghurt has never been greater — there are so many varieties of texture and flavour, it almost becomes a dessert in itself. But plain yoghurt has its place in baking, providing necessary acidity and depth of taste in baked goods.

Double Pink Lassi

SERVES 4

RASPBERRIES

1 cup	250 mL	raspberries, fresh or frozen

RHUBARB

1 1/2 cups	375 mL	rhubarb, chopped
1/4 cup	50 mL	sugar
3 Tbsp	45 mL	water

LASSI

1 1/2 cups	375 mL	ground almonds
1	1	cinnamon stick
2 cups	500 mL	milk
2 1/2 cups	625 mL	plain yoghurt
1 cup	250 mL	crushed ice
1/4 cup	50 mL	almond slices, toasted

A lassi is a refreshing Indian drink, almost like a milkshake, but the tartness of yoghurt adds a refreshing quality. This would be a great finish to a summertime meal al fresco, or after a spicy meal.

FOR RASPBERRIES, simmer berries with sugar for 5 minutes, purée and strain. Chill until ready to use.

FOR RHUBARB, simmer with sugar and water for 10 minutes until tender and purée. Chill until ready to use.

FOR LASSI, heat ground almonds and cinnamon stick with milk to just below a simmer. Stir occasionally and keep at low heat for 10 minutes. Strain milk through a fine strainer lined with cheesecloth, twisting cheesecloth to get every bit of juice out of almonds. Chill completely.

In a blender, purée chilled milk with yoghurt, rhubarb purée and 1/2 of raspberry purée with ice. Divide remaining raspberry purée among 4 tall glasses. Top up with lassi mixture. Garnish with toasted almond slices.

Frozen Yoghurt Lassi

The Double Pink Lassi can be easily spun into frozen yoghurt for an even more delectable summertime treat.

Prepare raspberry and rhubarb purées and almond milk (see page 124). Whisk together chilled milk, yoghurt, rhubarb purée and half of raspberry purée. Pour into an ice cream maker and churn according to manufacturer's instructions. Right before you stop the ice cream maker, drizzle in remaining raspberry purée and let blend just 10 or 15 seconds for a lovely raspberry ripple! Spoon into a container and freeze until firm.

NOTES

✧ Some specialty stores sell almond milk that can be used in place of making your own in this recipe. If you really like that almond flavour, add a little almond extract to give it a boost.

✧ Be sure to squeeze out every last drop of milk from the almond mixture. It's the last few drops that have the most intense taste!

✧ Low-fat yoghurt works just fine in this recipe, as does low-fat milk. Just think how healthy you're being!

✧ Yoghurt works as a 1:1 substitute for buttermilk in most recipes (once stirred, the consistency resembles buttermilk).

Sherry Yoghurt Cake with Glazed Oranges and Honey Mousse

CAKE

1/2 cup	125 mL	yoghurt
1/2 cup	125 mL	vegetable oil
1 Tbsp	15 mL	lime zest
1	1	egg
1/4 cup	50 mL	sweet sherry (Oloroso, Amontillado or Cream)
1 cup	250 mL	sugar
1 3/4 cup	425 mL	all purpose flour
2 tsp	10 mL	baking powder
1/4 tsp	1 mL	salt

HONEY MOUSSE
MAKES ABOUT 3 CUPS (750 ML)

2 tsp	10 mL	gelatin powder
3 Tbsp	45 mL	cold water
1	1	egg yolk
1/4 cup	50 mL	honey
1 1/3 cups	300 mL	whipping cream
2 Tbsp	25 mL	yoghurt
2 tsp	10 mL	sweet sherry

It's amazing what a little lime zest and sherry can do for a recipe. This is a relatively simple cake recipe, but the addition of sherry adds so much sophistication. Serving it with Honey Mousse and Glazed Oranges adds even more flair.

FOR CAKE, preheat oven to 400°F (200°C). Line bottom and sides of an 8-inch (20-cm) springform pan with parchment paper.

Whisk together yoghurt, oil, lime zest, egg and sherry. Whisk in sugar. In a separate bowl, sift flour, baking powder and salt. Stir into wet mixture until just blended. Scrape batter into prepared tin and bake for 20 – 25 minutes, until a tester inserted in the centre of the cake comes out clean. Cool in tin for 15 minutes, then turn out onto cooling rack.

FOR MOUSSE, soften gelatin in 2 Tbsp (25 mL) cold water and let sit while preparing egg base. Whisk egg yolk with honey and remaining 1 Tbsp (15 mL) cold water in a bowl over a pot of gently simmering water until pale and thickened, about 2 minutes. Whisk in gelatin to dissolve and allow to cool to room temperature.

Whip cream to soft peaks. While still whipping, add yoghurt and egg and honey mixture. Fold in sherry and pour into a dish to chill. Chill for at least 4 hours.

GLAZED ORANGES

MAKES ABOUT 1 1/2 CUPS (375 ML)

1 cup	250 mL	fresh orange juice
1/4 cup	50 mL	sugar
2	2	star anise
1 Tbsp	15 mL	cornstarch
3 Tbsp	45 mL	cold water
2	2	oranges

FOR GLAZED ORANGES, bring orange juice, sugar and star anise up to a simmer. Cook for 5 minutes, then spoon out star anise. Stir cornstarch with cold water and whisk into juice. Bring back up to a simmer and remove from heat. Peel oranges with a serrated knife and section, removing the membrane. Stir into orange syrup.

To serve, place a slice of cake on a plate, spoon glazed oranges over cake and onto plate and spoon a dollop of honey mousse on the side.

NOTES

⬧ I use sherry in all sorts of cooking and keep a bottle in the fridge all the time. It's my secret to the best caramelized onions — I add a shot right before I pull the onions off the stove.

⬧ The anise in the Glazed Oranges works to tie the flavour of the cake and the mousse together. The honey mousse is tasty on its own or with other spiced cakes or fruits. For a maple mousse, just replace the honey with pure maple syrup.

⬧ When making the oranges, the mixture will seem quite thick when it comes off the stove, but the addition of the orange segments will thin it as their juices are extracted by the heat.

Sour Cream

It is in my nature to love sour cream — my Slavic heritage decrees it!

Sour Cream Coffee Cake

MAKES 1 8-INCH (20-CM) SQUARE PAN
SERVES 9 TO 12

CAKE

1/2 cup	125 mL	unsalted butter, room temperature
1 cup	250 mL	sugar
2	2	eggs
1 tsp	5 mL	vanilla
1 cup	250 mL	sour cream
2 cups	500 mL	all purpose flour
1 1/2 tsp	7 mL	baking powder
1 tsp	5 mL	baking soda
1/4 tsp	1 mL	salt

TOPPING

1/4 cup	50 mL	golden brown sugar, packed
1 Tbsp	15 mL	all purpose flour
1 tsp	5 mL	cinnamon
1/2 cup	125 mL	walnut pieces
1 Tbsp	15 mL	unsalted butter, melted

My Mom used to make a square pan of sour cream coffee cake that would sit on the counter, loosely wrapped and with a butter knife left in the pan. Anyone strolling by could just lift up the plastic and cut a slice without being noticed.

FOR CAKE, preheat oven to 350°F (180°C). Cream butter and sugar until smooth. Add eggs one at a time, stirring well after each addition. Add vanilla and stir in sour cream. In a separate bowl, combine dry ingredients and stir into wet ingredients until just incorporated.

FOR TOPPING, combine all ingredients in a bowl. Scrape half the coffee cake batter into a greased 8-inch (20-cm) square cake pan and level. Sprinkle half the topping over cake and cover with remaining batter. Finish with topping and bake for 35–40 minutes, until a tester inserted in the centre of the cake comes out clean.

Serve warm or at room temperature.

NOTES

◇ This cake batter is more spreadable than pourable, so take a moment to make sure it sits evenly in the pan.

◇ Use regular sour cream, not low-fat, in baking for perfect results every time.

◇ Mix a few chocolate chips into the cake batter and the streusel topping for a little treat (I have to confess, I've also used butter-scotch chips!).

Sour Cream Apple Coffee Cake MAKES 1 8-INCH (20-CM) ROUND CAKE

To dress up this great cake a little, toss 2 cups (500 mL) of peeled and sliced Mutsu or Granny Smith apples in half of the crumble mixture. Prepare cake as on page 128 and scrape into a greased 8-inch (20-cm) round pan. Pour apples on top and finish with remaining crumble topping. Add an extra 10 minutes to the cooking time and you've got a perfect treat for tea time!

Passion Fruit Hotcakes with Sour Cream Ice Cream

PASSION FRUIT HOTCAKES

½ cup	125 mL	milk
¼ cup	50 mL	sour cream
2 Tbsp	25 mL	butter
1 tsp	5 mL	active dry yeast
¾ cup	175 mL	all purpose flour
1 Tbsp	15 mL	sugar
¼ tsp	1 mL	salt
1 Tbsp	15 mL	lemon zest
1	1	egg
		vegetable oil or food release spray, for frying
3	3	ripe passion fruits

SOUR CREAM ICE CREAM
MAKES ABOUT 3 CUPS (750 ML)

2 cups	500 mL	half-and-half cream
6 Tbsp	90 mL	sugar
1 Tbsp	15 mL	cornstarch
1 cup	250 mL	sour cream, full fat

Pancakes for dessert? Once you try this recipe, you'll make them for dessert and breakfast! These are yeast-raised hotcakes, almost like Russian blinis. The depth of flavour created by the yeast is irresistible. Warm hotcakes, fresh passion fruit and refreshing sour cream ice cream just cannot be refused!

FOR HOTCAKES, combine milk, sour cream and butter in pot on medium heat. Stir until butter is melted. Allow to cool until just around body temperature. Sprinkle yeast over surface of mixture and let stand 5 minutes.

In separate bowl combine flour, sugar, salt and lemon zest. Pour milk mixture into flour and stir until just combined. Cover tightly with plastic wrap and let stand in warm place for 1 hour. Whisk egg. Stir into batter to dissolve bubbles.

In heavy skillet over medium heat, add vegetable oil or spray. Add 1½ tsp (7 mL) of batter to skillet. Cook until bubbles disappear, then turn over. Remove from skillet when golden. Repeat with remaining batter. Hotcakes can be kept warm on a covered plate in a 200°F (95°C) oven.

FOR ICE CREAM, pour cream into a saucepan. Toss sugar and cornstarch together and whisk into cream. Heat on medium heat, stirring constantly until mixture thickens, about 5 minutes. Remove from heat and cool. Chill completely.

Stir sour cream into cream and churn in an ice cream maker according to manufacturer's instructions. Scrape into a container and freeze until firm.

To serve, cut passion fruit in half and scoop out seeds and pulp. Drizzle over hotcakes and top with Sour Cream Ice Cream.

NOTES
◇ When purchasing passion fruit, look for fruit that is soft and has a dark, very wrinkled skin. The riper the fruit, the sweeter and juicier the flavour.

◇ This ice cream is not overly sweet and works well with any other fruit dessert.

◇ This dessert has endless variations — fresh berries or peaches, warm sautéed bananas or pineapple, or even jam would make perfect accompaniments.

Whipped Cream

I think whipped cream qualifies as an ingredient itself because it's such a staple component in any bakeshop. In Europe, many kitchens have a machine that pours out whipped cream for baking, just like a soft ice cream machine. Wouldn't you love to have one of those at home!

Fruit Brûlées

MAKES 6 5-OUNCE (150-ML) SERVINGS

This is a brûlée not in the traditional sense of a cooked custard, but in the sense that it achieves the fantastic balance of fruit, cream and caramelized sugar. Warm fruit is topped with cold cream, and just as the cream starts to melt, you top it with hot caramelized sugar. As the sugar hits the cold cream, it petrifies into a crunchy topping. Seconds, anyone?

FOR CREAM, whip cream to soft peaks and stir in sugar. Chill until ready to serve.

FOR FRUIT, preheat oven to 400°F (180°C). Toss peaches, raspberries, blueberries and blackberries with superfine sugar and lemon zest and let sit for 10 minutes. Spoon into ramekins and bake for 8 – 10 minutes, just until hot. Remove from heat.

FOR SUGAR, while fruit is roasting, bring sugar, lemon juice and water up to a boil in a saucepan. Without stirring, cook sugar to a light golden brown, brushing the sides of the pan with water occasionally.

To serve, top hot fruit with whipped cream, and pour hot sugar over cream. As the warm fruit and hot sugar comes in contact with the cream, it will melt slightly into the fruit. Serve immediately.

CREAM

1 1/2 cups	375 mL	whipping cream
2 Tbsp	25 mL	sugar

FRUIT

2 cups	500 mL	peaches, sliced
1 cup	250 mL	raspberries
1 cup	250 mL	blueberries
1 cup	250 mL	blackberries
1/4 cup	50 mL	superfine sugar
1 tsp	5 mL	lemon zest

SUGAR

1/2 cup	125 mL	sugar
1 tsp	5 mL	lemon juice
3 Tbsp	45 mL	water

NOTES

✧ While the steps are simple in this recipe, timing is an issue. Have your cream whipped and fruit ready to go in the oven before you start caramelizing the sugar. If your sugar is ready before you are, cool it by setting the pot in a bowl of cold water and then re-warm over low heat, swirling gently until melted enough to pour.

✧ Use any combination of soft fruit — pineapple, mango or plum are all great choices.

✧ If whipped cream sits in the fridge for more than an hour or two, it starts to flop a little. Just give it a quick whisk and it will come back to life.

[Switch Up]

Fruit Brûlées with Candied Walnuts

CANDIED WALNUTS
MAKES 1 CUP (250 ML)

| 1 cup | 250 mL | walnut halves |
| 3 Tbsp | 45 mL | honey |

Adding candied walnuts just adds another level of complexity in taste without complicating the method. Prepare these in advance of assembling the Fruit Brûlées (page 131).

FOR WALNUTS, preheat oven to 350°F (180°C). Toss nuts with honey and spread onto a parchment-lined baking sheet. Bake for 12 – 15 minutes, stirring once until richly browned. Let cool. Sprinkle on top of prepared brûlées (page 131) and serve immediately.

Cannoli

SHELLS

3 cups	750 mL	all purpose flour
1 1/2 tsp	7 mL	sugar
		dash salt
1/2 cup	125 mL	unsalted butter, cool but not cold
2	2	eggs
1/2 cup	125 mL	Marsala wine
		vegetable oil, for frying

FILLING

1 cup	250 mL	dry ricotta
2/3 cup	150 mL	icing sugar
1/2 tsp	2 mL	cinnamon
1 tsp	5 mL	lemon zest
1 cup	250 mL	whipping cream
5 Tbsp	70 mL	semisweet chocolate, grated

"Leave the gun, bring the cannoli." We all recognize that line from *The Godfather*, but once you try these, you will appreciate why they were so valued in the movie!

FOR SHELLS, combine flour, sugar and salt. Cut in the butter until evenly blended. Whisk together eggs and wine and mix into flour and butter until it forms a dough. Turn out onto a lightly floured surface and knead to bring together. Wrap and let rest at room temperature for 20 minutes.

Roll out dough as thinly as possible, about 1/8 inch (3 mm) thick. Dock with a fork and cut into 3-inch (8-cm) circles. Scrap dough can be re-rolled to cut more discs. Keep discs covered when not using.

Heat oil to 350°F (180°C) (it should spit when a drop of water is added). Wrap disc around cannoli tube, and press where edges overlap. Immerse in oil and fry until golden brown. Place on a paper towel or cooling rack to drain for a moment, and before completely cooled, remove tube. Repeat with remaining discs, frying a few at a time. Cool completely before filling.

FOR FILLING, stir together ricotta with icing sugar, cinnamon and lemon zest until smooth. Whip cream to medium peaks and fold into ricotta. Fold in grated chocolate.

To assemble, fill a piping bag fitted with a star tip with cannoli filling. Pipe into shells, starting at middle and working out to each end. Cannoli can be topped with a little filling and a little more grated chocolate.

NOTES

⬦ You do need special cannoli tubes to make these properly. Most specialty kitchen shops carry them.

⬦ The cannoli dough should have the consistency of homemade pasta dough (not at all like pie pastry). In fact, it can be rolled through a pasta machine if you have one.

⬦ When using a piping bag, be sure to squeeze from the top of the bag. If you squeeze from the bottom, the warmth of your hand will alter the consistency of the filling. This applies to anything you might be piping — creams, mousses or icings.

Cream Cheese

Cream cheese can shine as the star ingredient in a dessert, the most obvious being cheesecake, but it can also be the secret ingredient in a tasty treat, in a pie crust or cookie dough. Cream cheese recipes are my favourite for licking the bowl and spoon when I'm finished baking.

Walnut Cream Cheese Rugalach

1 cup	250 mL	unsalted butter at room temperature
8 ounces	250 g	cream cheese at room temperature
3 cups	750 mL	all purpose flour
1/4 tsp	1 mL	salt
3/4 cup	175 mL	lightly toasted walnuts
1/2 cup	125 mL	dried cherries
1/2 cup	125 mL	sugar
1 tsp	5 mL	cinnamon
2 tsp	10 mL	cream (or sour cream)
1 tsp	5 mL	vanilla extract

These are a holiday staple around my house, and a fun recipe to make with kids.

Cream together butter and cream cheese until smooth. Add flour and salt and mix until dough just comes together. Wrap and chill dough for at least 2 hours.

Chop walnuts and dried cherries finely. Mix together with sugar, cinnamon, cream and vanilla extract until evenly blended.

Preheat oven to 350°F (180°C). Cut dough into 8 pieces, and shape each into rounds. On a surface lightly dusted with icing sugar, roll a ball into a disc, about 6–8 inches in diameter. Cut disc into 8 triangles. Sprinkle filling at widest end of each triangle. Roll each wedge from widest end, creating a croissant-like cookie. Pull ends together to touch and place on a parchment-lined baking sheet. Bake cookies for 15–20 minutes.

NOTES

✧ Apricot jam makes another great rugalach filling. Try prune, poppyseed or raspberry fillings as well.

✧ Rugalach means "little twists" in Yiddish, and they look like miniature croissants.

✧ Soft or firm cream cheese will work in this recipe.

Walnut Cream Cheese Rugalach with Port Steeped Figs

PORT STEEPED FIGS

SERVES 8

8	8	fresh figs
I cup	250 mL	port wine
2	2	cinnamon sticks

The elegance of delicate pastry with intense figs is a perfect ending to a meal.

Slice top of figs in an "x" without slicing all the way through to the bottom. Open fruit to expose their centres. Place in a pot closely together, pour port over figs and add cinnamon sticks. Heat on low for 15 minutes until warm. Remove from heat and let figs sit in port until ready to serve.

Serve figs in a shallow dish, drizzle with the port, with Walnut Cream Cheese Rugalach (page 134) on the side.

Perfect Cheesecake

MAKES 1 10-INCH (25-CM) CHEESECAKE
SERVES 12 TO 16

CRUST

I cup	250 mL	all purpose flour
I cup	250 mL	graham crumbs
4 tsp	20 mL	sugar
		dash salt
1/2 cup	125 mL	unsalted butter, melted

FILLING

2 1/2 lbs	1.25 kg	cream cheese, softened
1 3/4 cups	425 mL	sugar
3 Tbsp	45 mL	all purpose flour
I	I	vanilla bean
I Tbsp	15 mL	vanilla extract
I Tbsp	15 mL	lemon zest
1/4 tsp	I mL	salt
5	5	eggs at room temperature

SUGARED LEMON ZEST

2	2	lemons
1 1/4 cups	300 mL	sugar
I cup	250 mL	boiling water

What makes this recipe the perfect cheesecake is the 2 1/2 pounds (1.25 kg) of cream cheese! The additions of sugared lemon zest for the sides of the cake and sugared pansies on top make for a gorgeous presentable dessert, but the cake will taste no less delicious without the fancy trimmings.

FOR CRUST, preheat oven to 350°F (180°C). Combine flour, graham crumbs, sugar and salt in a bowl. Add melted butter and mix to an even crumbly texture. Press crust into a lightly greased 10-inch (25-cm) springform pan, pressing up the sides a bit. Bake for 12 – 15 minutes. Allow to cool.

FOR FILLING, reduce oven temperature to 300°F (150°C). Beat cream cheese until smooth and fluffy, scraping sides of bowl frequently. Gradually add sugar, scraping sides often. Add flour, scraped seeds from vanilla bean, vanilla extract, lemon zest and salt and mix well. Add eggs, one at a time, mixing well after each addition and scraping sides.

Scrape filling into springform pan. Place into a baking pan with edges, and fill pan with boiling water 1 inch (2.5 cm) up the sides. Bake cheesecake for 90 minutes with the oven door cracked open slightly. Allow cake to sit at room temperature for an hour before chilling. It is essential to chill overnight.

FOR SUGARED LEMON ZEST, slice off the top and tail of the lemons and score the lemons lengthwise about 5 times. Pull the scored peel off the lemons, as if peeling an orange.

Julienne (slice thinly lengthwise) the peel segments. Blanch the peel in a pot of boiling water for 2 minutes and drain (this cooks out the bitterness). Return zest to pot with 1 cup (250 mL) sugar and 1 cup (250 mL) boiling water and simmer until zest appears translucent, about 15 minutes. Drain well (you can reserve the syrup to poach fruits or brush onto a lemon loaf). Spread zest onto a parchment-lined baking sheet and let dry for 4 – 6 hours. Toss zest with remaining 1/4 cup (50 mL) sugar to coat. Zest will keep in an airtight container for up to 2 weeks.

SUGARED PANSIES

1	1	egg white
		pansies (or rose petals)
1/4 cup	50 mL	fruit sugar, (quick dissolve)

FOR SUGARED PANSIES, whisk egg white until foamy, but not fully whipped. Brush or delicately dip flowers with egg white and sprinkle with sugar. Set on a baking pan to dry. Flowers should last a few days in an airtight container.

To assemble, run a knife around edge of springform pan to loosen. Arrange sugared zest around outside edge of cheesecake and dot top with sugared pansies.

NOTES

⬦ The secret to a successful, smooth cheesecake — scrape down the sides of your mixing bowl often… then scrape it again.

⬦ A cracked cheesecake can be easily overcome with a few tricks. The water bath required in this recipe helps create a gentler cooking process. Baking with the oven door opened slightly will also help. If a further step is required, when the cheesecake is almost done, shut off the oven and let the cake cool in the oven. Be certain that the cake is room temperature before chilling (so as to avoid shocking it). If all else fails, blend 1/2 cup (125 mL) of sour cream with 1 Tbsp (15 mL) sugar, spread on top of the chilled cheescake, bake for 10 minutes at 350°F (180°C) and re-chill. No one will guess what hides beneath!

⬦ Cheesecakes slice easily with a hot, dry knife. Immerse a knife in hot water, wipe with a towel and slice.

⬦ I prefer the regular, full-fat variety of cream cheese in baking compared to low-fat. When you are craving that rich bite of cheesecake — that smoothness as you pull the creamy cake off your fork while humming at the same time — why sell yourself short by using low-fat?

nuts

WALNUTS | PECANS | PEANUT BUTTER | CASHEWS | MACADAMIA NUTS
ALMONDS | MARZIPAN

Walnuts

At our first home, I would curse the black walnut trees that grew in our backyard. The tannic outer shells of the walnuts would fall and make the soil so acidic that virtually nothing would grow except hostas. Now that we've moved, I realize that the trees had little to do with it — I am a horrific gardener. So now I speak only favourable things about walnuts.

I grew up eating walnuts because they were my Mom's favourite, and hardly a cookie or coffee cake was made without them.

Walnut Chocolate Brownies

MAKES 1 11 × 7-INCH (2-L) PAN
12 TO 20 BROWNIES

1 cup	250 mL	unsalted butter
1 cup	250 mL	cocoa powder
1³/₄ cups	425 mL	sugar
4	4	eggs, room temperature
2 tsp	10 mL	vanilla extract
1¹/₄ cups	300 mL	all purpose flour
1 tsp	5 mL	baking powder
¹/₂ tsp	2 mL	salt
²/₃ cup	150 mL	walnut pieces, toasted

Brownies — everybody's favourite! I have tried so many different brownie recipes, but I keep falling back to this one.

Preheat oven to 350°F (180°C) and grease an 11 x 7-inch (2-L) baking pan. Melt butter and pour into a larger bowl. Sift cocoa into butter and stir in. Stir in sugar. Add eggs to mixture, blending well after each addition. Stir in vanilla. In a separate bowl, combine flour, baking powder and salt (do not sift). Add to cocoa mixture and blend. Stir in walnuts. Pour into pan and bake for 35 minutes, until firm.

NOTES

✧ Toasting the walnuts before baking the brownies adds more dimension and flavour.

✧ Remember, the longer you bake your brownies, the "cakier" they become, so bake to your liking! The baking time I specified is for fudgy brownies, which is also why I don't sift the flour.

✧ For black forest brownies, try adding ¹/₃ cup (75 mL) dried cherries — they plump up as the brownies bake.

Walnut Chocolate Brownie Neopolitan

MAKES 1 8 × 4-INCH (1.5-L) LOAF
SERVES 8 TO 10

CHILLED HOT CHOCOLATE SAUCE
MAKES ABOUT 2¹/₂ CUPS (625 ML)

2 cups	500 mL	whipping cream
2 Tbsp	25 mL	cocoa powder
1 tsp	5 mL	vanilla extract
		dash salt
2	2	egg yolks
3 Tbsp	45 mL	sugar

There's only one thing better than chocolate brownies — chocolate brownies with ice cream! This terrine of strawberry ice cream sandwiched between 2 layers of brownies is a great summertime treat, especially with a Chilled Hot Chocolate Sauce!

Prepare Walnut Chocolate Brownie recipe (page 141) and cool. Thaw 2 cups (500 mL) strawberry ice cream for 5 minutes, just to soften. Remove brownie from pan and slice in half. Trim edges and place one half in an 8 × 4-inch (1.5-L) pan lined with plastic wrap. Spoon ice cream onto brownie in tin and spread into corners. Top ice cream with other trimmed half of brownie. Wrap and freeze until ready to serve (brownie should not freeze completely due to high sugar content).

FOR CHILLED HOT CHOCOLATE SAUCE, heat cream over medium heat with sifted cocoa powder, vanilla and salt. In a bowl, whisk together egg yolks and sugar. Gradually add hot cream to egg mixture, whisking constantly until all cream has been added. Return cream to heat and cook for 2 minutes, stirring until thickened. Strain and chill until ready to serve.

Slice brownie and serve with Chilled Hot Chocolate Sauce and Raspberry Sauce (see page 27) on the side.

Walnut, Fig and Brie Tart with Pear Sauce

CRUST

1³/₄ cups	425 mL	all purpose flour
1/3 cup	75 mL	lightly toasted and ground walnuts
2 Tbsp	25 mL	sugar
1/4 tsp	1 mL	salt
3/4 cup + 2 Tbsp	175 mL 25 mL	unsalted butter, cut into pieces and chilled
3 Tbsp	45 mL	cold water

FILLING

1 1/4 cups	300 mL	walnut halves
7 Tbsp	105 mL	honey
1/2 cup	125 mL	creamy ricotta cheese
6 ounces	175 g	brie cheese (triple crème is best!)
12	12	fresh figs

PEAR SAUCE
MAKES 1 CUP (250 ML)

2	2	ripe pears
1/4 cup	50 mL	honey
1	1	vanilla bean
1/2 cup	125 mL	white wine

NOTES

❖ The walnuts in the crust add a lot of moisture, which can make the dough soft and more challenging to roll (especially if the nuts are very fresh). You can press the dough into the pan instead of rolling if this is the case.

❖ The ricotta in the filling serves to hold the brie in place, so it doesn't melt away into nothingness, and because of its mild taste it doesn't interfere with the flavour of the brie.

❖ If fresh figs are not in season, pear slices make an excellent substitute.

This is a perfect ending to a meal when you want to serve something for dessert, but not something too sweet. As the cheese course increases in popularity, this also serves the cause. It is also perfect for a holiday buffet table because it presents so beautifully.

FOR CRUST, combine flour, walnuts, sugar and salt. Cut in butter to an even crumbly texture. Add 3 Tbsp (45 mL) cold water and mix just until dough comes together. If needed, add up to 1 more Tbsp (15 mL) water. Wrap and chill for an hour before rolling.

Preheat oven to 350°F (180°C). On a lightly floured surface, roll out dough to 1/4 inch (5 mm) thick. Line a 9-inch (23-cm) tart shell with crust and trim edges. Line tart crust with foil and weigh down with dried beans or rice. Bake for 15 minutes, then remove weights and foil and bake for 10 minutes more. Allow to cool.

FOR FILLING, toss walnuts in 2 Tbsp (25 mL) honey and spread onto a parchment-lined baking sheet. Bake for 10 – 12 minutes and let cool. Mix together ricotta and brie. Spread over the bottom of the tart shell. Cut figs into quarters and arrange, flesh-side up around tart. Sprinkle walnut halves over figs. Bake tart for 10 – 12 minutes, just to melt the cheese and warm the figs. While warm, drizzle remaining honey over tart.

FOR PEAR SAUCE, peel and dice pears, and cook with honey, scraped seeds from vanilla bean and wine until tender, about 15 minutes. Purée and strain sauce. Chill before serving.

Serve tart warm or at room temperature. Spoon sauce on the side of a slice of tart.

Pecans

Having spent a little time working in New Orleans, I have come to appreciate the value sweet, buttery pecans can add to dishes.

Pecan Scones

SCONES

3 cups	750 mL	all purpose flour
1/4 cup	50 mL	sugar
1 Tbsp	15 mL	baking powder
1/2 tsp	2 mL	salt
3/4 cup	175 mL	unsalted butter, cut into pieces and chilled
3/4 cup +1 Tbsp	175 mL +15 mL	milk
1/4 cup	50 mL	honey
2 tsp	10 mL	vanilla extract
3/4 cup	175 mL	pecans, lightly toasted and chopped

CINNAMON CREAM

1/2 cup	125 mL	whipping cream
2 Tbsp	25 mL	sour cream
2 Tbsp	25 mL	sugar
1/2 tsp	2 mL	cinnamon

A good scone recipe can't be beat.

FOR SCONES, preheat oven to 375°F (180°C). Place all dry ingredients in a mixing bowl, or in the bowl of an electric mixer fitted with the paddle attachment. Cut butter into dry ingredients until crumbly, but little bits of butter are still visible. Stir together 3/4 cup (175 mL) milk, honey and vanilla and add to dough. Mix just until dough comes together and add pecans.

Turn dough onto a lightly floured surface. Roll dough twice to a 1-inch (2.5-cm) thickness, each time folding in half (this is the secret to a flaky scone). Now roll dough to 3/4-inch (2-cm) thickness and cut desired shapes. Place on a greased or parchment-lined baking sheet and brush with remaining 1 Tbsp (15 mL) milk. Bake for 15 – 18 minutes, until tops are nicely browned.

FOR CINNAMON CREAM, whip cream to soft peaks and whisk in sour cream, sugar and cinnamon. Serve scones warm or at room temperature with cinnamon cream.

NOTES

❖ If serving the scones in the morning, you can prepare the dough the evening before, chill and then roll and bake in the morning.

❖ When making just for snacking, I just cut wedges of scones from a flattened disc of the dough, but when serving to guests I cut rounds for a prettier presentation.

❖ I like to use my hands when making scones, so I can really feel where the butter is. Rubbing the dough through my palms flattens the butter for flakier scones.

Glazed Pecan Scones with Autumn Compote

GLAZE

1 Tbsp	15 mL	milk
1 Tbsp	15 mL	maple syrup
1/4 cup	50 mL	icing sugar, sifted

AUTUMN COMPOTE
MAKES ABOUT 4 CUPS (1 L)

1	1	Mutsu (Crispin) or Granny Smith apple, peeled and diced
1	1	pear, peeled and diced
1	1	plum, pitted and diced
1/4 cup	50 mL	dried cherries
1/4 cup	50 mL	raisins
1 Tbsp	15 mL	lemon zest
3/4 cup	175 mL	sugar
1	1	cinnamon stick or 1 tsp (15 mL) ground cinnamon
1/4 tsp	1 mL	nutmeg
2 Tbsp	25 mL	brandy, optional

This is an autumn version of strawberry shortcake that is always well received when I have company over. It's a good finish to a brunch as well.

FOR GLAZE, whisk ingredients together and brush over scones after they come out of the oven and have cooled for about 5 minutes.

FOR AUTUMN COMPOTE, place all ingredients in a medium pot, and simmer for 10 – 15 minutes, until fruit is tender. Fruit can be served warm or at room temperature. Compote will keep in fridge for up to a week. Try on pancakes or waffles at breakfast!

To assemble, scones can be split and filled with cream and compote, or cream-filled scones can rest on top of compote. If you have a few remaining toasted pecans, sprinkle them on top.

Maple Pecan Tart

CREAM CHEESE PASTRY

1 cup	250 mL	unsalted butter at room temperature
6 ounces	175 g	cream cheese at room temperature
2 cups	500 mL	all purpose flour

FILLING

2/3 cup	150 mL	unsalted butter, melted
1 cup	250 mL	golden brown sugar, packed
4	4	eggs
3/4 cup	175 mL	maple syrup
2 tsp	10 mL	vanilla
		dash salt
3 cups	750 mL	pecan halves

This has been a part of my recipe repertoire for years and has always been a big seller.

FOR PASTRY, preheat oven to 375°F (180°C). In a mixer fitted with paddle attachment, cream together butter and cream cheese until smooth. Add flour and blend until dough comes together. Shape dough into a disc, wrap and chill for at least 1 hour.

On a lightly floured surface, roll out dough to 1/4 inch (5 mm) thick. Place dough into an 8-inch (20-cm) removable bottom tart shell or pie pan and trim edges. Press edges a little, so that dough rises just above the edge of the pan, about 1/4 inch (5 mm). Chill for 20 minutes.

FOR FILLING, whisk together all ingredients except pecans until smooth. Pour filling into chilled, unbaked tart shell. Arrange pecan halves on top of filling. Bake tart on a baking tray for 25–30 minutes, until filling doesn't jiggle when you shake it, and crust is golden brown. Allow tart to cool completely before cutting.

NOTES

❖ I like the cream cheese pastry for this tart because the tang of the cheese offsets the sweetness of the filling.

❖ It may seem silly to put your rolled tart crust in the fridge for just that 20 minutes, but letting the pastry "rest" will ensure that it stays tender and doesn't shrink as it bakes.

❖ As in making butter tarts, do not overmix the filling or it will soufflé and spill out of the pan.

Peanut Butter

There's something so basic and appealing about desserts made with peanut butter. It's as if the first taste of the salty-sweet combination allows us to revert back to our childhood, even if just for a moment or two.

The Ultimate Peanut Butter Cookie MAKES ABOUT 2 DOZEN COOKIES

¹/₂ cup	125 mL	unsalted butter at room temperature
¹/₂ cup	125 mL	sugar
¹/₂ cup	125 mL	golden brown sugar, packed
I	I	egg
I tsp	5 mL	vanilla extract
¹/₂ cup	125 mL	peanut butter (smooth or crunchy)
I ¹/₂ cups	375 mL	all purpose flour
I tsp	5 mL	baking soda
¹/₄ tsp	I mL	salt

I can recall the big brown mixing bowl I would pull out of my Mom's baking cupboard to make these cookies. I laugh at the size of it now, because it seemed so big at the time — my whole arm would reach in it!

Preheat oven to 350°F (180°C). Cream together butter and sugars until pale and fluffy. Beat in egg and vanilla. Stir in peanut butter. In a separate bowl, combine flour, baking soda and salt. Add to peanut butter mixture and blend in. Drop by table-spoonfuls onto an ungreased cookie sheet and crisscross mark them with a floured fork. Bake for 9 – 11 minutes, until cookies just start to colour around the edges.

NOTES

◊ Please add chocolate chips, butterscotch chips, chopped peanuts — whatever you choose will be a delicious addition!

◊ Using a fork to flatten cookies is classic, but try a butter stamp or cookie stamp for a different look.

Sweet Banana Peanut Butter Cookies   MAKES 12 SANDWICH COOKIES

1 Tbsp	15 mL	unsalted butter, room temperature
4¹/₂ tsp	22 mL	golden brown sugar, packed
1¹/₂ tsp	7 mL	sugar
1 Tbsp	15 mL	rum
		dash cinnamon
2	2	bananas, sliced
4 ounces	125 g	cream cheese, room temperature
¹/₂ cup	125 mL	smooth peanut butter

A bit different from your standard ice cream sandwich, these cookies are filled with a peanut butter and banana filling. Absolutely irresistible!

Prepare Peanut Butter Cookies (page 147). For filling, in sauté pan, melt butter over medium heat. Add sugars and increase heat to medium-high. Stir until melted and bubbling. Add rum (watch out for flames) and cinnamon. Stir in bananas to coat and set aside.

Cream together cream cheese and peanut butter until smooth. Mash bananas and add to cream cheese mixture until smooth. Chill for 20 minutes.

Fill between 2 peanut butter cookies to make sandwiches. Repeat with remaining cookies and refrigerate until ready to serve.

Peanut Butter Chocolate Cups MAKES 1 DOZEN TARTS

CRUST

¼ cup	50 mL	unsalted, roasted peanuts
¼ cup	50 mL	sugar
I cup	250 mL	all purpose flour
¼ cup	50 mL	cocoa powder
¼ tsp	I mL	salt
6 Tbsp	90 mL	unsalted butter, cut into pieces and chilled
3	3	egg yolks
I tsp	5 mL	vanilla extract

GANACHE

¾ cup	175 mL	whipping cream
6 ounces	175 g	bittersweet chocolate, chopped

FILLING

I ⅓ cups	325 mL	peanut butter (smooth or crunchy)
4 ounces	125 mL	cream cheese, room temperature
⅔ cup	150 mL	icing sugar, sifted
3 Tbsp	45 mL	condensed milk
I ⅓ cups	325 mL	whipping cream
I Tbsp	15 mL	vanilla extract

Be honest — you love those chocolate peanut butter cups, don't you? These tarts are as decadent and even more delicious than their original inspiration.

FOR CRUST, pulse peanuts in food processor with sugar, flour, cocoa and salt. Add butter and pulse in until even crumbly texture. Add egg yolks and vanilla and pulse just until dough comes together. Wrap in a disc and chill for 30 minutes. Press dough into greased muffin tins. Preheat oven to 350°F (180°C). Dock tart shells by marking with a fork and bake for 12 – 15 minutes until centre of shell is dry. Allow to cool.

FOR GANACHE, heat whipping cream to just below a simmer and pour over chopped chocolate. Let sit for I minute. Stir until evenly blended then spoon into prepared shells, reserving ¼ cup (50 mL) ganache for garnish.

FOR FILLING, beat peanut butter with cream cheese until smooth. Stir in icing sugar until smooth. Add condensed milk. Whip whipping cream with vanilla to soft peaks. Fold into peanut butter mixture. Spoon or pipe into tart shells.

To garnish, drizzle with remaining ganache (if it has cooled and set while preparing filling, melt in microwave for 15 seconds). Chill until ready to serve.

NOTES

◇ This is a great chocolate crust recipe, and is made so much easier because it is pressed into the pan, instead of being rolled.

◇ Pulsing nuts in a food processor with sugar or flour prevents the nuts from becoming paste, or in this case peanut butter.

◇ To save time, you can skip the ganache step (but remember what you'll be missing — mmmmm chocolate).

Cashews

Cashews are so naturally sweet, they're almost dessert in themselves. The sweet buttery taste is as distinctive as the C-shape. Because of the high fat content, make certain the nuts are very fresh when you buy them.

Cashew Baklava

MAKES 1 13 × 9-INCH (3.5-L) PAN

SYRUP

2 cups	500 mL	sugar
1 cup	250 mL	water
1 cup	250 mL	honey
3	3	whole cloves
1/2	1/2	lemon
1/2 tsp	2 mL	ground cardamom

BAKLAVA

1 1/2 cups	375 mL	unsalted cashews
1 1/2 cups	375 mL	walnuts
1/2 cup	125 mL	sugar
1 tsp	5 mL	ground cardamom
1/2 tsp	2 mL	cinnamon
1/4 tsp	1 mL	allspice
16	16	sheets phyllo pastry
1/3 cup	150 mL	unsalted butter, melted

On my ventures to St. Lawrence farmers' market while working in downtown Toronto, I would always stop at the Future Bakery booth for a piece of baklava, to give me the energy to keep shopping.

FOR SYRUP, put all ingredients in a pot and bring up to a simmer. Simmer for 10 minutes, stirring occasionally. Remove from heat and remove lemon and cloves. Allow to cool to room temperature.

FOR BAKLAVA, preheat oven to 350°F (180°C). Pulse cashews, walnuts, sugar and spices in a food processor until nuts are finely chopped. Brush 4 sheets of phyllo with butter, layering on top of each other (remember to keep unused phyllo covered under a damp cloth). Cut the phyllo in half and place one half over the other. Place the phyllo in the bottom of a 13 x 9-inch (3.5-L) greased baking pan, trimming edges as needed. Sprinkle phyllo with one-third of the nut mixture. Repeat process twice more with 4 sheets of pastry and sprinkling with nut mixture. Finish with last 4 sheets of phyllo. Score the top of the baklava into squares and/or triangles. Bake for 35–40 minutes, until golden brown.

While baklava is still hot, pour syrup over to coat. Refrigerate 4–6 hours (or overnight) before cutting.

Baby Baklavas

MAKES 16 BAKLAVAS

Just varying the technique for the baklava produces individual pastries, great for a tea tray or a host gift.

Prepare the syrup and filling as for Cashew Baklava (see page 150). Brush 1 sheet of phyllo with butter and fold in half. Lay wooden spoon lengthwise across phyllo sheet and roll up (remember to keep unused phyllo covered under a damp cloth). Scrunch dough towards end of spoon, and then slide off. Join ends of phyllo to create a circle. Place the phyllo in the bottom of a 13 x 9-inch (3.5-L) baking pan. Fill phyllo with 4^1/$_2$ tsp (22 mL) of the nut mixture. Repeat with remaining 15 sheets of phyllo pastry. Sprinkle remaining nut mixture on top of the 16 baklavas. Bake for 35 – 40 minutes, until golden brown.

While baklava is still hot, pour syrup over to coat. Refrigerate 4 – 6 hours (or overnight).

NOTES

❖ Did you know the cashew nut grows on the flower-end of a pear-shaped fruit? It has a very hard shell and is difficult to extract, hence its steep pricetag.

❖ I balance the richness (and cost) of cashews with walnuts in this recipe. Try your own mix of nuts.

❖ When brushing phyllo with butter, only the sheerest coat is needed, and the butter does not have to touch all the pastry.

Cashew Cookie Platter

Sometimes a formal dessert is not required after dining with guests. If serving coffee or after-dinner drinks, a plate of cookies is all that is needed. These elegant concoctions are a delightfully themed balance of texture and taste, but are delicious in their own right.

Cashew Madeleines

MAKES 24 MADELEINES

1 cup	250 mL	pastry flour
2 Tbsp	25 mL	unsalted cashews, lightly toasted
1/2 tsp	2 mL	baking powder
		dash salt
1/3 cup	150 mL	unsalted butter
3	3	eggs at room temperature
2	2	egg yolks
2/3 cup	175 mL	sugar
1 tsp	5 mL	vanilla extract
		icing sugar, for dusting
	OR	
2 ounces	50 g	chocolate, chopped (optional for dipping)
	OR	
1/2 cup	125 mL	chocolate chips

Pulse the flour and nuts in a food processor until nuts are as finely ground as possible. Sift flour with baking powder and salt (adding any nut pieces that may not fall through sieve). Repeat sifting.

Melt butter in a saucepan over medium heat. Let bubble and turn golden brown, 3–4 minutes. Remove from heat and cool to room temperature (no need to strain browned solids at bottom of pan — they add flavour!).

Whip eggs and egg yolks together on high speed to double the volume. Gradually add sugar while whipping, and continue until it's pale yellow and thick (whisk or beaters leave a ribbon when lifted). Beat in vanilla. Fold in flour gently. Stir a few tablespoonfuls of batter into butter and stir to combine. Fold butter mixture into batter and chill for 20 minutes.

Preheat oven to 375°F (190°C) and grease and flour madeleine (shell-shaped) molds. Dollop batter into each mold and bake for 12–15 minutes, until the centres of madeleines spring back when touched. Cool for 3 minutes then turn out onto a cooling rack.

Madeleines are traditionally dusted with icing sugar to finish, but can be dressed up by dipping in chocolate. Melt chocolate over a pot of gently simmering water, stirring constantly until smooth. Stir to cool to just below body temperature. Dip madeleines halfway in chocolate, shake off excess chocolate and set on a parchment-lined baking sheet. You can chill the madeleines for 5 minutes to help set chocolate, but they should be served at room temperature.

NOTES

◇ Madeleines are almost like little cakes and require a shell-shaped baking tin, available at most kitchen stores. If not an option, mini-muffin tins work just fine.

Cashew Brandy Snaps

¾ cup	175 mL	sugar
½ cup	125 mL	unsalted cashews, toasted and finely chopped
6 Tbsp	90 mL	all purpose flour
2 Tbsp	25 mL	lemon juice
2 Tbsp	25 mL	brandy
¼ cup	50 mL	unsalted butter, melted

NOTES

❖ Brandy snaps are a great addition to a serving of fresh fruit or berries, and are lovely with ice cream. The batter freezes exceptionally well.

Toss sugar, chopped cashews and flour to combine. Add lemon juice, brandy and melted butter and stir until batter is smooth. Chill for at least an hour. (Batter freezes well.)

Preheat oven to 350°F (180°C). On a silicone baking sheet or greased parchment paper, spread with a palette knife a circle of batter about 1½ inches (4 cm) across and about ⅛ inch (3 mm) thick. Repeat, leaving at least 2 inches (5 cm) between snaps. Bake for 7 – 9 minutes, rotating pan in oven halfway through baking. To curl snaps, remove pan from oven and let cool 1 minute. While still warm, remove snaps with palette knife and rest over a rolling pin to curl. For flat cookies, simply allow to cool completely on pan.

Cashew brandy snaps will keep for up to 3 days in an airtight container.

Cashew Crescent Cookies

2⅓ cups	575 mL	all purpose flour
1 cup + 2 Tbsp	250 mL 25 mL	unsalted cashews, toasted
		dash salt
1¼ cups	300 mL	unsalted butter, room temperature
⅓ cup	75 mL	sugar
		icing sugar for dusting

NOTES

❖ These crescent cookies are a holiday favourite with cashews, pistachios, walnuts or any buttery variety of nut.

Preheat oven to 350°F (180°C). Pulse flour, cashews and salt in food processor until cashews are finely chopped (but not ground) and set aside. Cream butter and sugar until fluffy. Stir in flour until dough comes together and is soft. Roll a tablespoonful of dough into a ball then into a log shape (the more you handle the dough, the more pliable it becomes and easier to shape). Bend into a crescent and place on a greased or parchment-lined baking sheet, leaving about 1½ inches (4 cm) between cookies. Bake for 15 – 20 minutes, until golden brown. Cool on baking sheet for 10 minutes then toss in icing sugar while still warm.

Macadamia Nuts

Not too long ago macadamia nuts were only available in tiny little jars that yielded only about a dozen nuts. Now you can even find them in the bulk section of the grocery store.

Macadamia Palmiers

³/₄ cup	175 mL	macadamia nuts
¹/₂ cup	125 mL	sugar
¹/₂ tsp	2 mL	cinnamon
1 pkg	1 pkg	puff pastry (2 sections per pkg)
¹/₂ cup	125 mL	unsalted butter, melted
		sugar, for dipping

MAKES 2 DOZEN

Palmiers, or "palm leaves," have a dual identity. Sometimes they function as a breakfast pastry, but they are also spotted on many a cookie or petits fours plate.

Pulse macadamia nuts in food processor with sugar and cinnamon to grind. On a lightly floured surface, stack both sections of puff pastry and roll out to 12 x 18 inches (30 x 45 cm) and ¹/₄ inch (3 mm) thick. Brush pastry with melted butter and sprinkle with macadamia sugar. Starting from each of the short sides, roll pastry inward so the two spirals meet in the centre. Brush along the seam where they meet with butter. If pastry is soft, chill for 15 minutes.

Preheat oven to 375°F (180°C). Slice ¹/₂-inch (5-mm) palmiers from roll and dip both sides in sugar, shaking off excess, and place on a parchment-lined baking sheet 2 inches (5 cm) apart. Bake for 10 minutes. Remove tray from oven and with a spatula, flip palmiers over and return to oven to bake another 10 – 12 minutes, until deep golden brown. Allow to cool.

Palmiers can be kept up to a week in an airtight container.

NOTES

◊ These pastries are a great use for scrap pieces of dough. Even leftover pie dough would work just fine.

◊ Flipping the palmiers halfway through baking will caramelize the sugar on both sides and make them flat and even-looking.

◊ Try making savoury versions as hors d'oeuvres — fill with grated cheese, olive tapenade, sundried tomato or pesto.

Chocolate Dipped Macadamia Palmiers

This step makes the palmiers perfectly suited to a cookie plate. Wrapped up, they make a great host gift.

Melt 4 ounces (125 g) of white or dark chocolate over a pot of gently simmering water, stirring constantly, or in microwave at medium heat, stirring every 15 seconds. Brush bottoms of Macadamia Palmiers (see page 154) with chocolate and place chocolate-side down on a parchment-lined baking tray and let set at room temperature or chill for 30 minutes, just to set.

Orange Macadamia Tarts with White Chocolate Ice Cream

PASTRY

1 1/2 cups	375 mL	all purpose flour
1 Tbsp	15 mL	sugar
1/4 tsp	1 mL	salt
1/2 cup	125 mL	unsalted butter, cut into pieces and chilled
3–4 Tbsp	45–60 mL	cold water

FILLING

1 1/3 cups	325 mL	macadamia nuts
1/4 cup	50 mL	dark brown sugar, packed
2 Tbsp	25 mL	golden corn syrup
2 Tbsp	25 mL	unsalted butter, melted
1	1	egg
2 tsp	10 mL	orange zest

WHITE CHOCOLATE ICE CREAM
MAKES ABOUT 3 CUPS (750 mL)

1 1/4 cups	275 mL	milk
4	4	egg yolks
6 Tbsp	90 mL	sugar
8 ounces	250 g	white chocolate, chopped
2 tsp	10 mL	vanilla
1 1/4 cups	300 mL	whipping cream

These tarts are like a tropical variation on a pecan or butter tart. There is less filling than a butter tart, because the macadamia nuts are so rich.

FOR PASTRY, combine flour, sugar and salt. Cut in butter until dough is an even, crumbly texture. Stir in cold water and mix just until dough comes together. Shape into a disc, wrap and chill for 15 minutes.

Preheat oven to 350°F (180°C). Cut pastry into 4 equal pieces. On a lightly floured surface, roll each piece to just less than 1/4 inch (3 mm) thick. Line 4 4-inch (10-cm) tartlette shells with pastry and trim edges. Chill for 10 minutes. Place shells on a baking tray, line with aluminum foil and fill with pie weights, rice or beans. Bake 15 minutes, then remove foil and weights and continue baking for 10 more minutes, until centres of shells are dry and edges are light brown.

FOR FILLING, pour 1/3 cup (75 mL) of macadamia nuts into each tart shell. Whisk brown sugar with corn syrup, melted butter, egg and orange zest until smooth. Pour over macadamia nuts. Swirl macadamia nuts around to coat. Bake tarts for 18–20 minutes, until set and nuts are light brown.

FOR WHITE CHOCOLATE ICE CREAM, heat milk to just below a simmer. Whisk together egg yolks and sugar. Gradually whisk hot milk into egg mixture. Return to pot and cook over medium-low heat, stirring with a wooden spoon until it coats the back of the spoon, remove from heat and strain. Stir in white chocolate and vanilla and chill completely.

Whip cream to soft peaks and fold into white chocolate mixture. Churn in an ice cream maker according to manufacturer's instructions. Spoon into a container and freeze until firm.

NOTES

◇ Most macadamia nuts come roasted and salted and this works fine in these recipes.

◇ Need a little more chocolate in your life? Add some chopped white chocolate chunks to the ice cream just as it finishes mixing in the ice cream maker.

◇ Try serving this dessert with a glass of orange liqueur.

Almonds

I think one of the key reasons I enjoy working with almonds so much is the variety of styles that can be purchased. Almonds are conveniently available whole, blanched, sliced, slivered and ground. No work needed on my part!

Orange Almond Biscotti

1½ cups	375 mL	whole almonds
5	5	eggs
1	1	egg yolk
2½ cups	625 mL	sugar
1 tsp	5 mL	vanilla extract
3½ cups	875 mL	all purpose flour
1 tsp	5 mL	baking powder
1 Tbsp	15 mL	orange zest
½ tsp	2 mL	cinnamon
		dash salt

1 egg, with 2 Tbsp (25 mL) cold water for egg wash

MAKES 4 TO 5 DOZEN

These cookies are indestructible. Keep them in a jar by the coffee maker or tea kettle for whenever you need a break.

Preheat oven to 350°F (180°C). Lightly toast almonds on a baking sheet for 10 minutes. Allow to cool.

Whisk together eggs, egg yolk, sugar and vanilla until sugar dissolves. In a separate bowl, stir together flour, baking powder, zest, cinnamon and salt (no need to sift). Add to egg mixture. Stir in almonds. Divide dough in half and roll each into a log shape on a floured surface. Logs should be about 15 inches (37.5 cm) long. Place each cookie log on a greased or parchment-lined baking sheet and press down with the heel of your hand to flatten. Brush tops of the biscotti dough with egg wash and bake for 25 minutes, rotating pan halfway through baking. Remove from heat and allow to cool for 15 minutes.

Reduce oven temperature to 325°F (160°C). Biscotti are easiest to slice while warm. Using a chef's knife, slice biscotti on an angle into ½-inch (1-cm) slices. Place face down on an ungreased baking sheet. Return cookies to oven for 20 minutes, or until they just start to colour a bit on the edges. They will feel soft when they come out of the oven, but will harden as they cool.

NOTES

❖ This dough is really quite sticky and sloppy. Use lots of flour to move the dough from table to tray if you need to, or shape the logs directly on the baking tray.

❖ Try these with hazelnuts, or substitute 1 cup (250 mL) of flour with 1 cup (250 mL) of sifted cocoa powder for chocolate biscotti.

Caramel Dipped Biscotti

CARAMEL

1 cup	250 mL	sugar
1 tsp	5 mL	corn syrup
1/4 cup	50 mL	water

Biscotti are traditionally softened for eating by dipping into your coffee. By coating the biscotti in caramelized sugar, you create a candy-like treat that also melts delicious caramel into your coffee while you stir it!

In a heavy-bottomed pot, bring sugar, corn syrup and water to a boil while covered. Once boiling, remove lid and let boil, brushing the sides of the pot once or twice with water, until the sugar turns light amber. Remove from heat and immerse pot into a bowl of cold water, to stop the sugar from cooking further.

Dip the Orange Almond Biscotti (see page 157) halfway into the hot sugar, swirling to coat. Place dipped biscotti on an oiled baking sheet and allow to cool completely.

Ricotta Almond Cake

MAKES 1 10-INCH (25-CM) CAKE
SERVES 12 TO 16

CAKE

4	4	eggs at room temperature
1 1/3 cups	325 mL	sugar
2/3 cup	150 mL	canola oil
2/3 cup	150 mL	creamy ricotta cheese
1/2 tsp	22 mL	lemon juice
1 Tbsp	15 mL	lemon zest
1 1/2 tsp	7 mL	rum
3/4 tsp	4 mL	vanilla extract
3/4 tsp	4 mL	almond extract
1 cup + 2 Tbsp	250 mL + 25 mL	ground almonds
1 1/4 cups	300 mL	all purpose flour
1 1/2 tsp	7 mL	baking powder
1/4 tsp	1 mL	salt

TOPPING

3/4 cup	175 mL	creamy ricotta cheese
1	1	egg
1/3 cup	75 mL	sugar
2 tsp	10 mL	lemon zest
1 tsp	5 mL	vanilla extract
2 Tbsp	25 mL	milk
1 cup	250 mL	sliced almonds

This cake conjures up images of dining on a patio as the sun is setting. Serve with fresh figs and pears to complete the Mediterranean moment.

FOR CAKE, preheat oven to 350°F (180°C). Butter and line with parchment a 10-inch (25-cm) springform pan. In a mixer fitted with the whisk attachment, beat eggs, sugar and oil on high speed until thick and pale, about 8 minutes. Add ricotta, juice, zest, rum, vanilla, and almond extract and mix until blended. Remove bowl from mixer.

In a separate bowl, sift together ground almonds, flour, baking powder and salt (adding back almonds that remain in sifter). Add to ricotta mixture in 3 additions, whisking by hand after each addition. Pour batter into springform pan and bake until a tester inserted in the centre comes out clean, about 40 – 45 minutes.

FOR TOPPING, blend together ricotta, egg, 1/4 cup (50 mL) sugar, zest and vanilla. Heat together milk and 2 Tbsp (25 mL) sugar. Pour over sliced almonds and toss to coat.

Allow cake to cool 6 – 8 minutes after coming out of the oven. Spread ricotta topping over cake and sprinkle with glazed almonds. Increase oven temperature to 375°F (190°C) and return cake to oven for 15 minutes, until almonds have browned. Cool cake completely before removing springform pan.

NOTES

⬧ This is one of the few occasions where I don't ask you to pre-toast your nuts before baking. You need the almonds to be untoasted to absorb liquid to bake into a moist cake.

⬧ Try stirring in raisins or candied fruit for a festive dessert

⬧ You need to let the cake cool for that 6 – 8 minutes before adding topping to stop the cooking process. The final step in the oven is just to toast the top layer of almonds.

Marzipan

Marzipan is a paste made of finely ground almonds and sugar, usually with the addition of a little bitter almond extract. Most commonly associated with fruitcakes, marzipan is actually quite a versatile ingredient. I used to make the mix myself, but found the store-bought variety far more consistent.

Marzipan Cake

MAKES 1 10-INCH (25-CM) CAKE
SERVES 12 TO 16

CAKE

1 cup	250 mL	unsalted butter, room temperature
1/2 cup	125 mL	sugar
1 cup	250 mL	marzipan
6	6	eggs
2 tsp	10 mL	lemon zest
1 tsp	5 mL	vanilla extract
1/2 tsp	2 mL	almond extract
1 cup	250 mL	all purpose flour
3/4 tsp	4 mL	baking powder
1/2 tsp	2 mL	salt

ALMOND CRUNCH

6 Tbsp	90 mL	icing sugar, sifted
1–2 Tbsp	15–25 mL	milk
1 cup	250 mL	sliced almonds, lightly toasted
		mixed berries, for garnish
		icing sugar for dusting

This is the moistest coffee cake ever! So soft and silky (all due to the marzipan of course), this would make a great layered birthday cake. I have also used this recipe to convert those who are afraid to use marzipan — it's so easy to make.

FOR CAKE, preheat oven to 350°F (180°C), butter and flour a 10-inch (25-cm) cake pan or springform pan and line bottom with parchment paper. With electric beaters, cream butter and sugar together. Cut marzipan (if marzipan is firm, soften in microwave for 30 seconds on high) into chunks and beat into butter mixture until smooth. Add eggs one at a time, mixing well after each addition and stir in lemon zest and extracts. In a separate bowl, sift together flour, baking powder and salt. Add to marzipan mixture and blend until smooth. Pour into prepared pan and bake for 35–45 minutes, until a tester inserted in the centre of the cake comes out clean. Allow to cool in pan for 20 minutes, then turn out onto a plate to cool completely.

FOR ALMOND CRUNCH, blend sifted icing sugar with milk until it's a brushable paste (add a little more milk or icing sugar to achieve desired consistency). Brush onto outside of cake (leaving top plain) and press almonds onto brushed surface. Top with mixed berries and dust with icing sugar.

Marzipan cake (without berries) will keep up to 5 days in an airtight container.

Marble Marzipan Cake

The combination of chocolate and almond together is absolutely spectacular, and easily achievable with this recipe. Simply divide the butter, sugar, marzipan and egg mixture from the Marzipan Cake (see page 160) in half and sift $1/2$ cup (125 mL) of flour with half the baking powder and salt in one bowl, and $1/2$ cup (125 mL) of cocoa powder with the remaining baking powder and salt into another bowl. Pour the chocolate layer in the bottom of the pan and the plain almond layer on top (no need to swirl the layers, they shift as they bake). Bake and finish as for Marzipan Cake.

NOTES

❖ Store marzipan in an airtight container at room temperature, or freeze.

❖ If your marzipan feels too dry (crumbles instead of tearing), knead a little water or liqueur, such as brandy or rum, into it until it becomes pliable.

❖ I like buying marzipan fruits at holiday time. An Italian bakery down the road from me makes absolutely beautiful confections — more works of art than candy!

Petits Fours

CAKE

1/2 cup	125 mL	unsalted butter, room temperature
1 1/4 cups	300 mL	sugar
1/2 tsp	2 mL	vanilla extract
1/4 tsp	1 mL	almond extract
2 cups	500 mL	pastry flour
1 Tbsp	15 mL	baking powder
1/4 tsp	1 mL	salt
3/4 cup	175 mL	buttermilk
6	6	egg whites

FOR ASSEMBLY

2/3 cup	150 mL	raspberry jam, stirred
8 ounces	250 g	rolling marzipan
1	1	egg white
1 1/2 lbs	750 g	rolling fondant icing
		decorations such as sugared flowers, silver candy balls, etc.
		paper cups, for serving

NOTES

⬦ This cake recipe is great when you are looking for a pure white cake, as it has no egg yolks.

⬦ Make certain your rolling surface is very clean before you roll marzipan or fondant icing. Any little crumb will stick and show up right where you don't want it!

⬦ I would occasionally get asked to make petit fours the colour of the bridesmaid dresses for bridal showers. To work colour into a frosting, I knead a bit of colour into a small piece of icing, then work it into the larger piece of icing a little at a time, to ease the colour in without any streaking.

⬦ Store your finished petits fours at room temperature. Sugar sweats if it is refrigerated, and your icing might melt if chilled.

These dainties are perfect for a bridal or baby shower. You can purchase rolling fondant icing at a specialty cake store and you can colour the fondant if you wish by adding a touch of colour paste and kneading into the fondant.

FOR CAKE, preheat oven to 350°F (180°C). Grease and line a 13 x 9-inch (3.5-L) cake pan with parchment, so that paper overhangs the long sides. Cream together butter and 1 cup (250 mL) sugar until fluffy. Add extracts and stir in. In a separate bowl, sift together flour, baking powder and salt. Add to butter mixture alternately with buttermilk. Whip egg whites until foamy, then gradually add remaining 1/4 cup (50 mL) sugar and whip to stiff peaks. Fold one-third of whites into batter then remaining two-thirds. Scrape batter into prepared pan and gently even out. Bake for 30 – 40 minutes, or until a tester inserted in the centre of the cake comes out clean. Allow to cool.

FOR ASSEMBLY, run a knife around edge of cake to loosen and lift out using the parchment paper to pull out. Brush a layer of stirred raspberry jam over cake. On a surface lightly dusted with icing sugar, roll out marzipan to 1/4-inch-thick (3-mm), 13 x 9-inch (32 x 23-cm) rectangle. Place over jam and trim edges. Rub surface of marzipan gently with your hand to ease out any possible air bubbles. Cut cake into 1 – 2-inch (2.5 – 5-cm) squares, or cut desired shapes with a cookie cutter (hearts or rounds).

Be certain that work surface and rolling pin are well cleaned. Cut off about 1/4 cup (50 mL) of fondant icing and shape into a ball (kneading will make it easier to roll). Roll on work surface lightly dusted with icing sugar to 1/4 inch (3 mm) thick. Brush top of petit four with egg white. Lift fondant disc and cover petit four completely, pressing down gently to eliminate any air bubbles. Trim edges at bottom of petits fours and rub entire surface of icing gently with fingertips to smooth out. Repeat process until all petits fours are covered. Clean fondant scraps (without cake crumbs) can be re-rolled many times. To decorate, brush bottom of decoration with a little egg white and fasten to petit four.

Petits fours will keep in an airtight container for 4 – 5 days.

other flavours

VANILLA | VANILLA BEANS | COFFEE | NUTMEG | CARDAMOM
OATS | PUMPKIN | COCONUT

Vanilla

This section deals with the classics — Vanilla Ice Cream and Vanilla Crème Brûlée. Who can resist a really good ice cream or custard? The cool creamy texture melts on your tongue and effortlessly slides down — you can't help but smile in contentment.

Vanilla Ice Cream

2 cups	500 mL	whipping cream
I cup	250 mL	milk
2	2	vanilla beans
9	9	egg yolks
⅔ cup	150 mL	sugar
		dash salt

MAKES ABOUT 4 CUPS (1 L)
SERVES 6 TO 8

This is a true custard ice cream — when I was a kid, my Mom would take me to her favourite ice cream stand, Hibbard's, in Lewiston for a huge ice cream cone. Half of it would end up dripping down my arm, but it was pure pleasure.

Heat cream and milk with the scraped seeds of vanilla beans (let pods steep in cream for extra flavour). Whisk together egg yolks, sugar and salt. When cream has come just to a simmer, remove bean pods. While whisking eggs, gradually add a little of the cream mixture at a time, until all has been mixed in. Reduce heat to medium low and return custard to heat, stirring until it thickens (or coats the back of the spoon). Remove from heat and strain. Chill completely.

Following manufacturer's instructions, make ice cream. Let firm up in freezer for an hour before scooping.

NOTES

❖ 2 Tbsp (25 mL) of vanilla extract can be used in place of vanilla bean in the ice cream recipe.

❖ I love picking up very ripe strawberries in season from a fruit-stand and adding them to this ice cream right before it finishes mixing for perfect Strawberries 'n' Cream ice cream.

Baked Alaskas

MERINGUE

4	4	egg whites
1/2 tsp	2 mL	cream of tartar
I cup	250 mL	sugar

A traditional Baked Alaska is a cake base topped with ice cream, smothered with meringue and baked briefly to brown. I have used the sugar cookie recipe (see Classic Crème Brûlée, page 169) as a base to create miniature versions of this grand dessert.

In a mixer or with an electric beater, whip egg whites and cream of tartar until foamy. Slowly add sugar and continue beating until whites hold stiff peaks.

To assemble, line a baking sheet with plastic wrap. Scoop 6 scoops of Vanilla Ice Cream (see page 167) onto sugar cookies and place on a baking sheet. Sprinkle with rum and re-freeze.

Using a spatula or palette knife, spread meringue over ice cream, pulling the spatula away to create curls or spikes (or a piping bag with a star tip makes easy work of this).

Keep frozen until ready to serve. Preheat oven to 400°F (200°C). Bake Alaskas for 2−3 minutes, until meringues just brown a little. Serve immediately.

Pumpkin Cranberry Loaf 186

Classic Crème Brûlée with Mini Sugar Cookies SERVES 6

VANILLA SUGAR

1	1	vanilla bean
2 cups	500 mL	sugar

CRÈME BRÛLÉE

3 cups	750 mL	whipping cream
2	2	vanilla beans
8	8	egg yolks
1/2 cup	125 mL	vanilla sugar or regular sugar
		dash salt

MINI SUGAR COOKIES
MAKES ABOUT 3 DOZEN MINI COOKIES

1/2 cup	125 mL	unsalted butter, room temperature
1 1/4 cups	300 mL	sugar
1	1	egg
3 Tbsp	45 mL	milk
1 tsp	5 mL	vanilla extract
2 cups	500 mL	all purpose flour
2 tsp	10 mL	cream of tartar
1 tsp	5 mL	baking soda
		dash salt
		sugar, for coating

NOTES

❖ Whipping the egg yolks and sugar together for the crème brûlée creates a fluffy, melt-in-the-mouth consistency that translates into a light yet rich end result.

❖ Try pouring the chilled custard mixture over fresh blueberries or raspberries and then bake.

❖ These sugar cookies are great all purpose cookies. Dip them in coloured sugars for a little flair.

Using vanilla sugar just builds on the fragrance and flavour of this recipe. If you do not have any made, regular sugar works just fine.

FOR VANILLA SUGAR, put vanilla bean in sugar and leave for two weeks.

FOR CRÈME BRÛLÉE, heat cream with the scraped seeds from vanilla beans and add pods to the cream until just below a simmer.

In a mixer fitted with the whisk attachment (or with an electric mixer), whip egg yolks, vanilla sugar and salt until pale and thick. With mixer on low speed, pour hot cream (with pods removed) into egg mixture, stopping to scrape down sides occasionally. Strain and chill completely. Brûlée mix can be made up to 2 days in advance.

Preheat oven to 350°F (180°C). Place 6 5-ounce (150-mL) ramekins (or shallow brûlée dishes) in a pan with at least a 1 1/2-inch (4-cm) lip. Open oven door and place pan on door. Give brûlée mix a stir and pour into cups. Pour boiling water around cups to come up halfway to the ramekins. Bake brûlées for 45–55 minutes, until they no longer jiggle when tapped. Remove from water bath and chill for at least 3 hours before serving.

To serve, heat broiler. Sprinkle tops of custards with vanilla sugar and broil for 1 minute or use a butane kitchen torch.

FOR MINI SUGAR COOKIES, preheat oven to 350°F (180°C). Cream together butter and sugar. Stir in egg, milk and vanilla. Sift together flour, cream of tartar, baking soda and salt and stir in. Shape small teaspoonfuls of cookie dough into balls and roll in sugar. Place on a greased baking sheet and press down with palm of your hand. Bake for 15 minutes and remove from pan to cool.

Vanilla Beans

Vanilla beans are truly something special. The pod of a climbing tropical orchid plant, they have to be harvested at a very specific time and fermented before they are ready for us to use.

Vanilla Jam Muffins

MAKES 12 MUFFINS

These are a jelly-doughnut type of a muffin. Inside each softly scented vanilla muffin is a raspberry jam filling just waiting to drip out onto the front of your shirt!

FOR MUFFINS, preheat oven to 350°F (180°C). Heat milk with scraped seeds and pod of vanilla bean over medium-low heat about 15 minutes, to infuse flavour. Remove vanilla pod and let milk cool to room temperature. Whisk sugar, oil and eggs into cooled milk. In a separate bowl, sift together flour, baking powder, nutmeg, salt and cinnamon. Add to milk mixture and blend just until incorporated (do not overmix). Fill greased muffin tins ²/₃ full with batter. Stir raspberry jam to soften and spoon a tablespoonful into centre of each muffin.

Top with remaining muffin batter and bake for 35−45 minutes, until even light golden brown on top. Let muffins cool in tin for 15 minutes, then turn out to cool completely.

FOR DIP, brush tops of muffins with melted butter and dip into a mixture of sugar and cinnamon. Store muffins in an airtight container for 2−3 days or freeze and warm in oven or microwave to serve.

MUFFINS

1¹/₂ cups	375 mL	milk
1	1	vanilla bean
1¹/₂ cups	375 mL	sugar
²/₃ cup	150 mL	vegetable oil
2	2	eggs
3¹/₂ cups	875 mL	all purpose flour
1 Tbsp	15 mL	baking powder
1 tsp	5 mL	nutmeg
1 tsp	5 mL	salt
¹/₂ tsp	2 mL	cinnamon
¹/₂ cup	125 mL	raspberry jam

DIP

¹/₄ cup	50 mL	unsalted butter, melted
¹/₄ cup	50 mL	sugar
¹/₂ tsp	2 mL	cinnamon

NOTES

✧ Vanilla beans respond best to heating to draw out the most flavour. You could use 1 Tbsp (15 mL) of pure vanilla extract in place of the vanilla bean and skip the heating of the milk.

✧ Use a firm jam for this recipe so the filling doesn't explode out of the muffins as they bake.

✧ Be careful not to overmix your muffin batter. If you have muffins that have pointy caps to them, then they have been overmixed. I prefer blending by hand as a precaution.

Vanilla Jam Fritters

Playing on the doughnut idea, these fritters become a great late-night snack or maybe an early morning one.

Fill a medium saucepan with enough vegetable oil to come up 2 inches (5 cm) in the pot. Heat to 350°F (180°C) (or when water spits and bubbles when a drop is added). Drop table-spoonfuls of batter, as prepared for Vanilla Jam Muffins (page 170), carefully into oil and fry about 5 minutes, turning over halfway through cooking. Remove with a slotted spoon and let drain on paper towels.

To fill with jam, poke a skewer into one end of the fritter and twirl a little to create an opening. Fill a piping bag fitted with a small tip with stirred jam and insert into fritter opening. Fill with jam and dust with icing sugar to finish. Serve fresh (within 4 hours).

Vanilla Chocolate Éclairs

PASTRY CREAM

2 cups	500 mL	milk
1	1	vanilla bean
8	8	egg yolks
1/4 cup	50 mL	sugar
5 Tbsp	70 mL	cornstarch
		dash salt
2 Tbsp	25 mL	unsalted butter
1 Tbsp	15 mL	brandy (optional)
1/4 cup	50 mL	whipping cream

ÉCLAIRS

1/2 cup	125 mL	milk
1/2 cup	125 mL	water
7 Tbsp	105 mL	unsalted butter
1 Tbsp	15 mL	sugar
1 tsp	5 mL	salt
1 1/2 cups	375 mL	bread flour
5 – 6	5 – 6	eggs, at room temperature

If you've never had a homemade éclair, then you haven't lived! Forget fake whipped cream — the density of a rich vanilla pastry cream filling in an egg-y pastry topped with a shiny chocolate glaze is unbeatable.

FOR PASTRY CREAM, bring milk and scraped seeds and pod of vanilla bean to a simmer over medium heat. In a bowl, whisk together egg yolks, sugar, cornstarch and salt. Whisking egg mixture constantly, gradually add milk, a ladle at a time, to the egg mixture until all the milk has been added. Pour mixture back into pot and return to medium heat. Whisking vigorously, bring mixture up to a simmer. Due to the cornstarch, pastry cream will thicken quickly, about 3 – 4 minutes. Remove from heat and strain. Stir in butter (this will help halt the cooking process). Stir in brandy, cover surface of pastry cream with plastic wrap and chill completely. Whip cream to medium peaks and fold in. Chill until ready to assemble.

FOR ÉCLAIRS, preheat oven to 400°F (200°C). Heat milk, water, butter, sugar and salt and bring up to a simmer. Sift flour and add all at once. Stir mixture over medium heat for 2 minutes. By hand or with a mixer fitted with the paddle attachment, add eggs one at a time, blending completely before adding additional egg. To know if you should add the sixth egg, lift a spoon (or the paddle) from the paste. If it "sheets" or leaves batter as you lift it then it does not need egg. If it still feels tight (is hard to pull away) then add the extra egg.

CHOCOLATE GLAZE

1¼ cups	300 mL	icing sugar, sifted
4 tsp	20 mL	cocoa powder, sifted
1 tsp	5 mL	corn syrup
2–3 Tbsp	25–45 mL	milk or water

Fit a pastry bag with a large plain piping tip. Fill bag and pipe 4-inch-long (5-cm) lines of paste onto a parchment-lined baking sheet, leaving at least 2 inches (5 cm) between each (secure the edges of the parchment to the pan by sticking it with a little of the paste). After all the dough has been piped, touch the finishing point of each éclair with a finger dipped in water, to flatten the point the tip has left. Bake éclairs for 12 minutes at 400°F (200°C). Do not open oven yet! Reduce heat to 360°F (185°C) and bake for an additional 8 minutes, until éclairs are rich golden brown. Allow to cool before filling.

Fill piping bag with a medium plain tip with chilled pastry cream. Insert tip into a long end of éclair and fill until cream stops at end of éclair. Continue filling all éclairs.

FOR CHOCOLATE GLAZE, stir together icing sugar and cocoa powder. Stir in corn syrup with milk until it's a smooth, pourable consistency. Dip éclair tops in glaze and let set on a cooling rack to dry. Keep éclairs chilled until ready to serve.

NOTES

◇ Using bread flour gives your éclairs more "puff," leaving more room for creamy filling!

◇ Store vanilla beans in an airtight container. A fresh vanilla bean should be very flexible.

◇ Keep your vanilla bean pods after the seeds have been scraped. For Vanilla Sugar see page 169. It's great stirred into coffee or baking for extra vanilla scent.

Coffee

Coffee desserts are perfect for the truly addicted — caffeine and sugar all in one! I even use coffee for added flavour in breads.

Mocha Bites

1 cup	250 mL	unsalted butter, room temperature
1/2 cup	125 mL	icing sugar, sifted
1/4 cup	50 mL	espresso
4 tsp	20 mL	vanilla
2 1/4 cups	550 mL	all purpose flour
1/4 cup	50 mL	cocoa powder
1/4 tsp	1 mL	salt
		sugar, for coating

Another recipe from my Mom — I got hooked on these one day as we were visiting over the holidays. We spent an hour chatting over cups of coffee and when I looked down, the plate of cookies had disappeared.

Preheat oven to 325°F (160°C). Cream together butter and icing sugar until smooth. Stir in espresso and vanilla. Sift in all purpose flour, cocoa and salt and mix until dough comes together. Turn dough onto a board lightly dusted with icing sugar. Divide dough in half and shape into logs. Slice dough on an angle in 1/2-inch (1-cm) slices. Place cookies upright on a parchment-lined baking sheet and bake for 20 minutes.

While warm, toss cookies gently, two at a time, in sugar and allow to cool.

NOTES

✧ If you don't have an espresso maker at home, purchase a shot of espresso at your neighbourhood coffee shop.

✧ Coffee is the world's favourite hot beverage — we consume over 15 billion cups a year! So it stands to reason that we need something to eat to go with our coffee, right?

Mocha Sundae

COFFEE SAUCE

MAKES 1²/₃ CUPS (400 ML)

1¹/₂ cups	375 mL	yoghurt
¹/₄ cup	50 mL	sugar
1 Tbsp	15 mL	cocoa powder
¹/₄ cup	50 mL	espresso
1 tsp	5 mL	vanilla
		chocolate or coffee ice cream

This is a fast recipe for a grown-up type of sundae. Great served with Mocha Bites (page 174).

Mix together yoghurt, sugar, cocoa powder, espresso and vanilla until smooth.

Scoop ice cream into dishes, top with sauce, and serve with mocha bites on the side.

Coffee and Doughnuts

COFFEE POTS DE CRÈME

MAKES 12 MINI POTS DE CRÈME OR 6 5-OUNCE (150-ML) RAMEKINS

1/3 cup	75 mL	espresso
1 1/2 cups	375 mL	whipping cream
1	1	vanilla bean
6	6	egg yolks
1/2 cup	125 mL	sugar

DOUGHNUTS

MAKES 12 TO 18 DOUGHNUTS

1 1/4 cups	300 mL	milk
2 1/2 tsp	12 mL	dry active yeast
1/2 cup	125 mL	sugar
3 1/2 cups	875 mL	all purpose flour
2	2	eggs
1 tsp	5 mL	salt
4 Tbsp	60 mL	unsalted butter, softened
1/2 tsp	2.5 mL	vanilla
1/4 tsp	1.25 mL	nutmeg
		icing sugar, for dusting

Playing on a classic combination, these rich, chilled coffee custards are a delicious contrast to warm New Orleans-style beignets.

FOR COFFEE POTS DE CRÈME, preheat oven to 350°F (180°C). Heat espresso with cream and scraped seeds from vanilla bean. While heating, whisk together yolks and sugar. Gradually add hot cream to egg mixture, whisking constantly. Place 12 espresso cups into a baking pan and pour custard mixture in. Pour boiling water around cups, coming up halfway. Bake for 30 – 40 minutes, until custard no longer jiggles when cup is tapped. Chill for 3 hours before serving.

FOR DOUGHNUTS, heat milk to just above body temperature and stir in yeast and sugar. Mix in remaining ingredients except icing sugar, and blend in a mixer for 5 minutes. Place dough in an oiled bowl, cover and let rise 1 hour.

On a lightly floured surface roll out dough to 3/4 inch (2 cm) thick. Cut dough into 2 x 2-inch (5 x 5-cm) squares and place on a baking sheet. Let rest for 10 minutes.

Heat a pot with 2 inches (5 cm) of vegetable oil over medium high heat. You will know the oil is hot enough when a drop of water sizzles when added to oil. Fry doughnuts a few at a time, cooking both sides until a rich brown colour, about 4 minutes for each side. Drain well. After cooling slightly, dust with icing sugar.

NOTES

❖ Since doughnuts are ideally eaten fresh, you can make and cut the dough ahead of time and chill, and cook the doughnuts at the last minute.

❖ It is the nutmeg that gives these doughnuts that distinctive, recognizable flavour.

❖ You can prepare these custards in regular-sized coffee cups for a dessert on their own (or maybe with a few mocha bites on the side).

Nutmeg

Nutmeg is like the viola or oboe in the symphony of spices. It rarely gets a solo, but is essential in performance. It has a subtle, background flavour that builds substance in a dessert. It is most closely associated with cool weather flavours like apples and, of course, eggnog, but it can also work in moderation with light lemon notes.

Apple Nutmeg Dumplings

MAKES 6 DUMPLINGS

These apple dumplings are quite different from the puff pastry-wrapped apples you see these days. An easy-to-make pastry covers apples filled with raisins, then a fragrant syrup is poured around and over the pastry. Surprisingly, this does not produce a soggy dumpling because the pastry absorbs the liquid and fluffs up.

FOR PASTRY, combine flour, sugar and salt. Cut in butter to an even crumbly texture. Add egg yolk and water and blend just until dough comes together. Wrap in plastic wrap and chill for 15 minutes.

FOR FILLING, peel and core apples. Mix 4 Tbsp (60 mL) sugar with 1/2 tsp (2 ml) cinnamon, nutmeg and dash of cloves. Dip apples in mixture to coat. In a separate bowl, combine raisins with breadcrumbs, remaining 2 Tbsp (25 mL) sugar, 1/2 tsp (2 mL) cinnamon and brandy.

Roll out pastry on a lightly floured surface into a rectangle 1/4 inch (5 mm) thick, about 20 x 12 inches (50 x 30 cm). Trim edges of dough and cut into 6 squares. Place an apple in the centre of each square and fill middle of apple with raisin filling. Wet edges of pastry squares and bring corners up to meet at top of apple and pinch together. Place dumplings in an ungreased baking dish (quite close together) and preheat oven to 375°F (190°C).

FOR SYRUP, bring water, sugar and spices to a simmer for 5 minutes. Remove from heat and stir in butter (this can be prepared ahead of time). Pour over dumplings. Bake for 45 minutes, until golden brown on top. Serve warm.

PASTRY

2 cups	500 mL	all purpose flour
2 Tbsp	25 mL	sugar
3/4 tsp	4 mL	salt
1 cup	250 mL	unsalted butter, cut into pieces
1	1	egg yolk
3 Tbsp	45 mL	water or milk

FILLING

6	6	small apples such as Macintosh or Spy
6 Tbsp	90 mL	sugar
1 tsp	5 mL	cinnamon
1/2 tsp	2 mL	nutmeg
		dash cloves
1/2 cup	125 mL	raisins
3 Tbsp	45 mL	breadcrumbs
2 Tbsp	25 mL	brandy

SYRUP

1 1/2 cups	375 mL	water
1 cup	250 mL	sugar
1 tsp	5 mL	cinnamon
1/2 tsp	2 mL	nutmeg
3 Tbsp	45 mL	unsalted butter

Apple Dumplings with Crème Anglaise

CRÈME ANGLAISE
MAKES 1¹/₃ CUPS (325 ML)

1 cup	250 mL	half-and-half cream
¹/₂	¹/₂	vanilla bean, or 1 tsp (5 mL) vanilla extract
2	2	egg yolks
3 Tbsp	45 mL	sugar

This sauce is a great addition to a regular baked apple as well.

Bring cream with scraped seeds of vanilla bean to just below a simmer. Whisk together egg yolks and sugar. Gently whisk cream into egg mixture and return to pot. With a wooden spoon over medium-low heat, stir sauce until it coats the back of a spoon, about 4 minutes. Strain and chill.

To serve, spoon Crème Anglaise over warm Apple Nutmeg Dumplings (see page 177).

NOTES

◇ Use fresh nutmeg, if available. Even if you don't use nutmeg often, the whole nut will keep far longer than grated.

◇ I like using Macintosh apples in this recipe because they get so squishy and tender when they bake.

◇ Nutmeg pops up in many dishes — the French use it in savoury applications such as Bechamel sauce, potato and spinach dishes.

Nutmeg Lemon Roulade

CAKE

6	6	eggs, separated
3/4 cup	175 mL	sugar
2 Tbsp	25 mL	unsalted butter, melted
1 Tbsp	15 mL	fancy molasses
1 tsp	5 mL	vanilla extract
2 tsp	10 mL	lemon zest
2/3 cup	150 mL	all purpose flour
2 Tbsp	25 mL	cornstarch
1 tsp	5 mL	baking powder
1 tsp	5 mL	nutmeg
1 tsp	5 mL	cinnamon
1/4 tsp	1 mL	salt
1/2 tsp	2 mL	cream of tartar
2 Tbsp	25 mL	sugar
		icing sugar, for rolling

FILLING

1 cup	250 mL	whipping cream
1 cup	250 mL	icing sugar, sifted
2 Tbsp	25 mL	lemon juice
1 tsp	5 mL	lemon zest
2 cups	500 mL	good quality mascarpone cheese
		icing sugar, for garnish
		lemon zest curls, for garnish (optional)

NOTES

◈ Rolling the jelly roll warm will set its shape so it won't crack when rolled after filling. A tea towel can be used in place of parchment for rolling (to prevent the rolled cake from sticking to itself).

◈ If you have extra lemon filling, pipe it on top of the roulade for garnish, or double the filling recipe to ice the cake completely.

◈ Did you know that nutmeg increases the effects of alcohol — maybe that's why we like it in our eggnog?

A fancy name for jelly roll, this cake has a smooth lemon cream filling that plays against the spiced cake nicely. This could double as a yule log at holiday time.

FOR CAKE, preheat oven to 350°F (180°C). Line a 15 x 10-inch (2-L) jelly roll pan with parchment paper, grease and flour, being certain to shake off excess. In a mixer fitted with the whisk attachment or with electric beaters, whip egg yolks and 3/4 cup (175 mL) sugar until mixture holds a ribbon when whisk is lifted. Stir in melted butter, molasses, vanilla and lemon zest. In a separate bowl, sift flour, cornstarch, baking powder, nutmeg, cinnamon and salt and fold into egg yolk mixture. Whip egg whites with cream of tartar until frothy, then add 2 Tbsp (25 mL) sugar and continue whipping to stiff peaks. Fold one-third of whites into batter until almost incorporated, then fold in remaining two-thirds. Spread onto prepared pan and bake for 15–18 minutes, until cake springs back when gently pressed.

Remove cake from oven and loosen edges from pan. Dust cake generously with icing sugar, cover with a sheet of parchment, top with another pan (if you have one) and flip over onto work area. Peel off parchment from jelly roll and dust top generously with icing sugar. Starting from a long side, roll up cake with parchment and let cake cool. This will set the jelly roll shape.

FOR FILLING, whip cream and icing sugar to soft peaks. Stir lemon juice and zest into mascarpone. Fold cream into mascarpone mixture.

To assemble, unroll sponge cake and spread with filling, leaving a gap of about 2–3 inches (5–8 cm) at the end. Roll up cake, being gentle so as not to push out filling (but some will move forward). Dollop remaining filling on top along length of cake, dust with icing sugar and garnish with lemon curls.

Cardamom

Cardamom is a relatively new spice in my pantry. My husband is of Icelandic background, and his mum always kept it in her cupboard for desserts like Vinetarta, a prune shortbread torte.

The light peppery sharpness of cardamom is a surprise on the palate and adds great zip to very sweet desserts, fruits and custards.

Cardamom Sugar Cookies

1 cup	250 mL	unsalted butter, room temperature
$^3/_4$ cup	175 mL	sugar
1	1	egg
1$^1/_2$ tsp	7 mL	vanilla extract
2 cups	500 mL	all purpose flour
$^3/_4$ tsp	4 mL	ground cardamom
$^1/_2$ tsp	2 mL	salt
$^1/_4$ tsp	1 mL	nutmeg

These are great cut-out cookies. Get creative and use whatever shapes you wish. Even better, get the kids to do it while you put your feet up for 10 minutes.

Beat butter and sugar together by hand or in a mixer, until pale and fluffy. Blend in egg and vanilla extract. In a separate bowl, stir together flour, cardamom, salt and nutmeg. Stir into butter mixture until just combined. Gather dough together, shape into 2 discs, wrap and chill until firm, about 1 – 2 hours, or freeze until ready to use (then thaw overnight in fridge).

Preheat oven to 325°F (160°C). On a lightly floured work surface, roll out first disc of dough to just less than $^1/_4$ inch (5 mm) thick. Cut out desired shapes and lift with a spatula onto a parchment-lined baking sheet. Roll second disc, saving all scraps to re-roll for more cut-outs. If you choose, add sprinkles or other decorations before baking. Bake for 12 – 15 minutes, until edges of cookies just begin to brown. Let cool before removing from tray.

Cookies will keep in an airtight container for up to 2 weeks.

NOTES

◇ Cardamom is a member of the ginger family, hence its subtle bite.

◇ This is a good recipe to make and store as dough in the freezer for emergency situations, such as scraped knees, a sad movie or a rough day at school or the office.

◇ Try cutting out doughnut-shaped cookies, with a hole in the centre. Bake until almost done, then fill centres with crushed hard candy and bake until melted. When candy sets up, you'll have stained glass cookies.

Glazed Cardamom Sugar Cookies

1 cup	250 mL	icing sugar, sifted
3 Tbsp	45 mL	milk
		decorator's sugar

A glaze adds polish and shine to these treats. Top with decorator's sugar for a little extra sparkle.

FOR GLAZE, combine icing sugar and milk and whisk until smooth. Brush Cardamom Sugar Cookies (see page 180) with glaze, sprinkle with decorator's sugar and allow to dry on a cooling rack for 1 hour.

Cardamom Crème Caramel

2¹/₂ cups	625 mL	sweetened coconut
2 cups	500 mL	sugar
2 Tbsp	25 mL	water
6	6	eggs
2 cups	500 mL	milk
I cup	250 mL	coconut milk
3 Tbsp	45 mL	all purpose flour
I tsp	5 mL	vanilla extract
I tsp	5 mL	ground cardamom

Making a good crème caramel is an extremely satisfying task, as it is truly a classic dessert. We have become accustomed, I find, to the rich density of crème brûlée, but a crème caramel has a lighter, more egg-y taste as it is prepared with milk and whole eggs versus cream and egg yolks.

Preheat oven to 325°F (160°C). Toast coconut lightly on a baking sheet for 6 – 8 minutes, stirring once while toasting. Cool and pulse in food processor until fine. Set aside.

Increase oven temperature to 375°F (190°C). In a sauté pan, melt I cup (250 mL) sugar over high heat with 2 Tbsp (25 mL) water. Cook the sugar without stirring until golden brown (about 3 – 4 minutes) and pour into an ungreased 9-inch (23-cm) round cake pan. Swirl sugar around bottom to coat. Place pan in a baking dish with a 2-inch (5-cm) lip.

In a large bowl, whisk eggs. Add remaining I cup (250 mL) sugar, milk, coconut milk, flour, sweetened coconut, vanilla and cardamom and whisk until well blended. Pour over caramelized sugar and carry to oven door. Pour boiling water around pan, coming up at least halfway and place carefully in oven. Bake for 55 – 60 minutes until a tester inserted in the centre comes out clean. Remove pan from water bath and let cool for 30 minutes.

Cardamom crème caramel can be served warm, but is delicious if chilled for 4 hours before serving. To serve, run a palette knife around the outside edge of the custard and invert the pan over a plate and lift.

NOTES

◇ This is a crème caramel with a built-in crust. The coconut floats to the surface as the custard bakes, creating a crust once inverted.

Oats

Oat crops thrive in a cool, moist climate which is why they are a staple in the Canadian baking cupboard (and on the breakfast shelf, too).

Oatmeal Cookies

MAKES ABOUT 2 DOZEN

2/3 cup	150 mL	unsalted butter, room temperature
1 cup	250 mL	dark brown sugar, packed
1	1	egg
1 Tbsp	15 mL	vanilla
1 Tbsp	15 mL	fancy molasses
1 cup	250 mL	all purpose flour
1/2 tsp	2 mL	baking powder
1/2 tsp	2 mL	salt
1/2 tsp	2 mL	baking soda
1/2 tsp	2 mL	cinnamon
1/4 tsp	1 mL	nutmeg
1 1/2 cup	375 mL	oats
1 cup	250 mL	raisins

Who doesn't like oatmeal cookies? A good basic recipe can be easily personalized by the addition of your favourite extras: raisins, chocolate chips, walnuts, cranberries.

Preheat oven to 375°F (190°C). Cream together butter and brown sugar until smooth. Add egg and blend. Stir in vanilla and molasses. In a separate bowl, combine flour, baking powder, salt, baking soda and spices. Add to butter mixture and mix in. Add oats and raisins and stir just until oats are coated with cookie batter. Drop tablespoonfuls onto a greased or parchment-lined baking sheet and bake for 7–9 minutes, until cookies start to brown around the edges and lose their shine.

Cookies will keep up to a week in an airtight container.

NOTES

◇ Bake with regular or quick-cook oats, but not instant. They will dissolve into a recipe too quickly. The more an oat is processed, the less nutritional value it has.

◇ Add a good mix of extras including nuts, dates and a little coconut and you've got a great hermit cookie. Just keep in mind that the more treats you add, the less the cookies will spread as they bake.

◇ It's the brown sugar and molasses in this recipe that keep the cookies moist and chewy.

Oatmeal Cookie Ice Cream Sandwiches

Here is another simple cookie conversion that, if at all possible, improves on the already close-to-perfect.

FOR SANDWICHES, press a $^1/_2$-cup (125-mL) scoop of ice cream between 2 Oatmeal Cookies (see page 183). Roll edges of ice cream in lightly toasted walnut crumbs and chill until ready to serve.

Oat Blueberry Crisps with Whiskey Oat Cream

FRUIT

4 cups	1 L	blueberries
3 cups	750 mL	peeled and diced pears
1 cup	250 mL	sugar
1/4 cup	50 mL	cornstarch
2 tsp	10 mL	orange zest

CRISP TOPPING

1/2 cup	125 mL	corn flake crumbs
1/2 cup	125 mL	oats
1/2 cup	125 mL	dark brown sugar, packed
1/2 tsp	2 mL	cinnamon
1/4 tsp	1 mL	allspice
1/4 tsp	1 mL	salt
6 Tbsp	90 mL	unsalted butter, melted
1 cup	250 mL	pecan halves, roughly chopped

WHISKEY OAT CREAM
MAKES 2 CUPS (500 ML)

1/4 cup	50 mL	oats, regular or quick-cook
1 cup	250 mL	whipping cream
2 Tbsp	25 mL	honey
4 1/2 tsp	22 mL	whiskey

Crisps are probably the most self-explanatory style of dessert. Oats are the traditional topper, but the addition of pecans adds an extra "crispness."

FOR FRUIT, preheat oven to 350°F (180°C). Combine blueberries in a pot with pears. In a bowl, mix sugar and cornstarch together to blend and add to blueberries, along with orange zest. Bring mixture just up to a boil, stirring regularly and pour into 8 5-ounce (150-mL) ramekins.

FOR CRISP TOPPING, combine corn flake crumbs, oats, brown sugar, spices and salt. Stir in melted butter until mixture is evenly blended. Add chopped pecans and mix. Spread crisp topping over fruit. Place baking dish on a baking sheet (to catch any drips) and bake for 30 – 35 minutes, until edges are bubbly and crisp topping is a rich brown. Allow to cool 20 minutes before serving.

FOR WHISKEY OAT CREAM, toast oats in a small pan over medium-low heat for 5 minutes, stirring often. Remove from heat and cool. Whip cream to soft peaks and fold in honey and whiskey. Fold in 2 Tbsp (25 mL) cooled oats.

To serve, dollop oat cream over warm crisps and garnish with remaining toasted oats.

NOTES

✧ Of course, any combination of fruit works well. After blueberry, I think tart cherry crisp is my favourite.

✧ The whiskey oat cream is also known in Scotland as "Cranachan." The toastiness in the oats is delicious, and the texture softens as the oats sit in the spiked cream. Try layering this with fresh berries for an easy alternate dessert.

✧ Another secret revealed! Using corn flake crumbs makes for an "über-crisp." Unbelievably crisp, nothing will make this dessert go soggy.

Pumpkin

You can always tell when autumn has arrived in my neck of the woods, because what were once green fields are barren except for the bright dots of scattered pumpkins.

Sweeter and denser than squash, pumpkin is perfect in desserts. There's also the simple reason that spices are often paired with pumpkin — it's a combination that can't be beat.

Pumpkin Cranberry Loaf

MAKES 1 9 × 5-INCH (2-L) LOAF

2 cups	500 mL	all purpose flour
1 tsp	5 mL	baking soda
1 tsp	5 mL	baking powder
1 tsp	5 mL	salt
1/2 tsp	2 mL	cinnamon
1/2 tsp	2 mL	cloves
1/2 tsp	2 mL	ginger
1/2 cup	125 mL	unsalted butter, room temperature
1 cup	250 mL	sugar
2	2	eggs
1 cup	250 mL	canned pumpkin purée
1 Tbsp	15 mL	orange zest
1 tsp	5 mL	vanilla
1 cup	250 mL	orange, juice
1 1/2 cups	375 mL	cranberries, fresh or frozen

The pumpkin purée ensures a moist loaf every time.

Preheat oven to 325°F (160°C). Sift together flour, baking soda and powder, salt and spices and set aside. In a medium bowl, cream together butter and sugar until light and fluffy. Add eggs, one at a time, and stir in pumpkin purée, orange zest and vanilla. Stir in orange juice. Add dry ingredients in 2 additions and blend just until incorporated. Fold in cranberries. Spoon batter into greased loaf pan and bake in centre of oven for 60 – 75 minutes until a tester inserted into the loaf comes out clean. Allow to cool before slicing.

NOTES

❖ If roasting fresh pumpkins, cut in half, scoop out seeds and dock skin with a fork. Bake flesh-side-down on a baking sheet at 350°F (180°C) for about 30 minutes, until soft. Allow to cool, scoop out flesh and purée until smooth. Freeze if not using immediately. It thaws easily in the microwave.

❖ This loaf bakes at a lower-than-usual temperature because it is a wet batter. The moisture will be slowly absorbed without scorching the outside of the loaf.

❖ My favourite way to eat this loaf is warm from the oven and slathered with sweet butter.

Pumpkin Cranberry Loaf with Crystallized Ginger Syrup

CRYSTALLIZED GINGER SYRUP

MAKES 1¹/₃ CUPS (325 ML)

¹/₂ cup	125 mL	white wine
¹/₂ cup	125 mL	water
1 cup	250 mL	sugar
2 tsp	10 mL	fresh grated ginger
2 Tbsp	25 mL	crystallized ginger, finely chopped
4¹/₂ tsp	22 mL	cornstarch
1 Tbsp	15 mL	cold water

This clear, fragrant syrup brings out the spice component of the loaf. Try it on vanilla ice cream as well.

In a small pot, stir together wine, water, sugar and gingers and bring up to a simmer.

Whisk together cornstarch with cold water and whisk into syrup. Stir glaze until shiny and bubbling. Remove from heat.

Syrup can be served warm or cool and keeps in the fridge for up to a week.

To serve, pour crystallized ginger syrup over slices of Pumpkin Cranberry Loaf (page 186).

Pumpkin Mousse with Molasses Cookies SERVES 10 TO 12

PUMPKIN MOUSSE

1 tsp	5 mL	gelatin
1/4 cup	50 mL	cold water
4	4	egg yolks
1 cup	250 mL	sugar
2 cups	500 mL	pumpkin purée
2 Tbsp	25 mL	brandy or Calvados
1 tsp	5 mL	cinnamon
1/2 tsp	2 mL	ginger
1/4 tsp	1 mL	cloves
1 3/4 cups	425 mL	whipping cream
1 Tbsp	15 mL	vanilla

MOLASSES COOKIES

MAKES 2 TO 3 DOZEN COOKIES

1/2 cup	125 mL	unsalted butter, at room temperature
1 1/2 cups	375 mL	sugar, plus extra for dipping
1/4 cup	50 mL	fancy molasses
1	1	egg
2 cups + 2 Tbsp	500 mL + 25 mL	all purpose flour
1/4 tsp	1 mL	salt
1 tsp	5 mL	baking soda
1 tsp	5 mL	ginger
1/2 tsp	2 mL	cloves
1/2 tsp	2 mL	cinnamon

This pumpkin mousse is fantastic served on its own but when paired with chewy molasses cookies it is the epitome of autumn.

FOR PUMPKIN MOUSSE, soften gelatin in 2 Tbsp (25 mL) of the cold water. In a metal bowl over a pot of simmering water, whisk egg yolks, sugar and remaining 2 Tbsp (25 mL) water until it doubles in volume and holds a ribbon when whisk is lifted (about 5 minutes). Remove from heat and stir in gelatin.

Place egg mixture in a mixer fitted with the whisk attachment and beat until cooled (another 5 minutes). Fold in pumpkin, brandy and spices and chill until cool, but not set, about 1/2 hour.

While mousse base is chilling, whip cream to soft peaks and add vanilla. Fold into mousse in 2 additions and chill until ready to serve.

FOR MOLASSES COOKIES, preheat oven to 350°F (180°C). In a medium bowl, cream together butter and sugar until light and fluffy. Add molasses and stir in egg. In a separate bowl, blend together flour, salt, baking soda and spices; add to butter base and blend until smooth.

Place some sugar in a small bowl. Shape cookie dough into 1 1/2-inch (4-cm) balls and toss into sugar. Place on a greased or parchment-lined baking sheet. Flatten cookies with your hand or the bottom of a glass. Bake cookies for 12 – 15 minutes, until lightly browned around the edges. Remove cookies from pan to cool. Cookies can be stored for up to 5 days in an airtight container.

To serve, place a cookie on a plate. Dollop a large spoonful of mousse on top of cookie.

NOTES
◇ Pour this mousse into a baked pie shell for a Pumpkin Chiffon Pie. Great for Thanksgiving.

◇ Using fancy molasses produces a sweeter, milder cookie versus the sharper blackstrap molasses, which has an almost bitter edge. I like to use blackstrap in my breads for colour and depth of flavour.

◇ I like to serve this dessert with a little drizzle of caramel on the plate and a few slices of fresh apple.

Coconut

Like banana desserts, I like to use coconut in baking when I need a hint of warm weather. The texture that grated coconut adds to baked goods is certainly unique. In fact, I often find myself snacking on it by the handful.

Macaroons

MAKES 2 1/2 TO 3 DOZEN

4	4	large egg whites
1 1/3 cups	325 mL	sugar
1/3 cup	75 mL	condensed milk
		dash salt
1 tsp	5 mL	vanilla extract
1 tsp	5 mL	almond extract
2 1/2 cups	625 mL	coconut
1/4 cup	50 mL	flour

These aren't the crunchy concoctions that crumble as soon as they touch your lips. These macaroons are the chewy, delectable sort that are more candy than cookie!

In a heavy saucepan stir together the egg whites, sugar, condensed milk, salt, vanilla, almond extract and coconut. Sift in flour and stir the mixture until it is combined well. Cook the mixture over moderate heat, stirring constantly, for 5 minutes. Increase the heat to moderately high and cook the mixture, stirring constantly, for 3 – 5 minutes more, or until it has thickened and begins to pull away from the bottom and sides of the pan. Transfer the mixture to a bowl, let it cool slightly at room temperature, then chill completely before baking.

Preheat oven to 300°F (150°C). Drop heaping teaspoons of the batter 2 inches (5 cm) apart onto greased or parchment-lined baking sheets and bake the macaroons on centre rack of the oven for 20 – 25 minutes, or until they are pale golden. Transfer the macaroons to a cooling rack.

Macaroons will keep up to 10 days in an airtight container.

NOTES

◇ Sweetened or unsweetened coconut makes no difference in this recipe. I usually use sweetened because that's what's usually in my pantry.

◇ Store unused coconut in the freezer. Keep it well-wrapped as it easily picks up other scents around it.

Cocoa Macaroons

By replacing the $^1/_4$ cup (50 mL) of flour in the Macaroons (page 189) with $^1/_4$ cup (50 mL) of cocoa powder, the result is an even more decadent cookie. Make some plain and some chocolate for variety on your next cookie plate.

NOTES FOR COCONUT CHIFFON CAKE >>

◇ This is a true chiffon cake, which went out of fashion after the 1960s (and I don't know why). It is so light tasting, stays perpetually moist, and is great on its own just dusted with icing sugar. Let's make it trendy again!

◇ This whipped cream stabilizing method is a great pastry chef trick. I use it on cakes and pies when I know it won't be served for at least 4 hours. The cream will hold its body for up to 24 hours this way.

◇ When toasting coconut, don't wait until all the coconut is browned. I pull it out of the oven when the edges of the coconut on the tray have colour and when just the top layer is toasted. The flavour is more subtle that way.

Coconut Chiffon Cake

CAKE

2¼ cups	550 mL	pastry flour
1½ cups	375 mL	sugar
2 tsp	10 mL	baking powder
1 tsp	5 mL	salt
1 cup	250 mL	coconut, toasted unsweetened
½ cup	125 mL	canola or vegetable oil
7	7	large eggs, separated
3	3	egg whites
¾ cup	175 mL	water
2 tsp	10 mL	vanilla extract
1 tsp	5 mL	coconut extract
1 Tbsp	15 mL	cream of tartar

LEMON CURD

⅓ cup	50 mL	lemon juice
3	3	eggs
1	1	egg yolk
½ cup	125 mL	sugar
1 tsp	5 mL	lemon zest
½ cup	125 mL	unsalted butter

COCONUT CREAM ICING

¼ cup	50 mL	icing sugar
2 tsp	10 mL	cornstarch
1 cup	250 mL	whipping cream
½ tsp	2 mL	vanilla
½ tsp	2 mL	coconut extract
1 cup	250 mL	sweetened coconut
		toasted coconut, for garnish

Truly spectacular, this dessert combines a light, fluffy chiffon cake with a lemon filling, topped with a cream frosting. Admire quickly after you've made it because it won't last long.

FOR CAKE, preheat oven to 325°F (160°C). In a large bowl, combine flour, all but 2 Tbsp (25 mL) of sugar, baking powder, salt and coconut. Make a well in the centre and add oil, egg yolks, water, vanilla and coconut extract. Beat until smooth. In a mixer fitted with the whisk attachment or with electric beaters, whip egg whites until frothy. Add cream of tartar and beat until soft peaks form. Beat in 2 Tbsp (25 mL) remaining sugar until stiff peaks form. Gently fold one-third of the egg whites into batter, then fold in remaining two-thirds. Pour batter into ungreased tube pan. Run a knife through batter to burst any air bubbles and bake for 1 hour or until cake springs back when touched (do not open oven door until at least 50 minutes have passed). Invert pan and cool for ½ hour. Loosen sides with a long metal spatula and remove core of pan.

FOR LEMON CURD, whisk together lemon juice, eggs, yolk, sugar and zest in a bowl over a pot of gently simmering water. Add butter and whisk steadily until curd becomes thick, pale and creamy, 10 – 15 minutes. Remove from heat and cover with plastic wrap resting directly on curd. Chill until ready to use.

FOR COCONUT CREAM ICING, refrigerate bowl and beater for 15 minutes. In a small saucepan, combine icing sugar and cornstarch and gradually stir in ¼ cup (50 mL) of the whipping cream. Bring to a boil, stirring constantly, for a few seconds. Scrape into small bowl to cool to room temperature. Add vanilla and coconut extract. Whisk remaining whipping cream to soft peaks. Add cornstarch mixture, whisking constantly, until stiff peaks form. Fold in coconut.

Cut cake into 3 layers. Spread half of the lemon curd on the bottom layer and place a layer of cake on top. Repeat with remaining curd and cake, ending with cake. Using an offset spatula, spread coconut cream icing generously over entire cake. Garnish with a light sprinkling of toasted coconut.

Bibliography

Better Homes & Gardens New Cookbook, Revised edition. Meredith Publishing Company, New York, 1962.

Davidson, Alan. *The Penguin Companion to Food*. Penguin Books, Toronto, 2002.

Friberg, Bo. *The Professional Pastry Chef: Fundamentals of Baking*, 4th edition. John Wiley & Sons, Inc., Toronto, 2002.

Gisslen, Wayne. *Professional Baking*, 3rd edition. John Wiley & Sons, Inc., Toronto, 2001.

Greenspan, Dorie. *Baking with Julia*. William Morrow & Company, Inc., New York, 1996.

Greenspan, Dorie. *Desserts by Pierre Hermé*. Little, Brown & Company, Toronto, 2001.

Lawson, Nigella. *How to Be a Domestic Goddess: Baking and the Art of Comfort Cooking*. Alfred A. Knopf Canada, Toronto, 2001.

Murdoch Books. *The Essential Baking Cookbook*. Whitecap Books Ltd., North Vancouver, 2000.

Murdoch Books. *The Essential Dessert Cookbook*. Whitecap Books Ltd., North Vancouver, 2000.

Olson, Anna & Michael. *The Inn on the Twenty Cookbook*. Whitecap Books Ltd., North Vancouver, 2000.

Ramsay, Gordon. *Gordon Ramsay's Just Desserts*. Quadrille Publishing Ltd., London, 2001.

Slater, Nigel. *Marie Claire Cookbook*. Mitchell Beazley, London, 1993.

Index

About the Author

◇ ◇ ◇ Anna Olson greatly enjoys living in Niagara, Ontario, with her husband, Michael, and two beagles, Oscar and Priscilla. When she is not working on the set of *sugar*, Anna spends her time teaching cooking classes, writing for various publications, and developing recipes and products. She also spends time working with the Niagara Women's Enterprise Centre, which offers hospitality training and employment counseling for women who might not otherwise have such opportunities.

The bounty of Niagara is an endless source of inspiration for new recipes for both Anna and Michael, who is a chef professor at Niagara Culinary Institute. The tender fruits, wine industry and other harvests give them a limitless supply of ideas and they enjoy cooking at home together.

Anna is also an avid reader and shopper, and has been known to spend many hours in local libraries expanding her mind and in stores reducing her wallet.